RETIREMENT AND INCOME

GARLAND REFERENCE LIBRARY
OF SOCIAL SCIENCE
(VOL. 142)

RETIREMENT AND INCOME
*A National Research Report
of Behavior and Opinion
Concerning Retirement, Pensions,
and Social Security*

Conducted by
Louis Harris & Associates, Inc.

GARLAND PUBLISHING, INC. • NEW YORK & LONDON
1984

Library of Congress Cataloging in Publication Data
Main entry under title:

Retirement and income.

  (Garland reference library of social science ; v. 142)
  1. Retirement income—United States. 2. Old age
pensions—United States. I. Louis Harris and Associates.
II. Series.
HD7105.35.U6R47 1984   331.25′2′0973   82-49183
ISBN 0-8240-9142-6 (alk. paper)

Printed on acid-free, 250-year-life paper
Manufactured in the United States of America

Johnson&Higgins

95 Wall Street

New York, New York 10005

DR. D. A. CHEKKI Ph.D.
Department of Sociology
University of Winnipeg
Winnipeg, R3B 2E9 CANADA

February 1979

Dynamic changes in American society are prompting a searching reevaluation of the nation's retirement patterns and systems. Decisions being made today will have serious implications for the American public — with truly major impact on the labor force, capital formation, corporate health, tax policy, Social Security and all private and public pension systems.

It is imperative that the policymakers formulating these decisions and the people affected thereby, both in the private and public sector, have available to them all the relevant information it is possible to obtain. Accordingly, we recently commissioned a nationwide survey to obtain a sharper focus on retirement problems and what to do about them. Business leaders, policymakers and other interested people will find the survey results most useful in the developing dialogue on these issues.

Richard I. Purnell
Chairman

Robert V. Hatcher, Jr.
President

A nationwide survey of the attitudes of employees, retirees and business leaders toward pensions and retirement.

PREFACE

The past decade has seen the emergence of major changes in social and economic forces directly affecting retirement. Reaction to these pressures has already produced significant legislation such as ERISA, sweeping amendments to Social Security taxes and benefit levels, changes in sex discrimination statutes, and moves toward non-mandatory retirement.

This is a fast paced ongoing process. Long-term pressures generated by the shift in the age and sex composition of the labor force will be magnified and accelerated by the more immediate pressures caused by an over-heated inflationary economy. The future will witness additional major changes in the American retirement system to accommodate these pressures –- changes in legislation, in employment practices, in retirement patterns and in the systems used to fund and pay retirement income.

Johnson & Higgins believes these coming changes, and the direction they will or should take, must be hammered out in the real world and not developed solely through theoretical think-tank studies of what is best for America. An essential step in the real world is an examination of the attitudes of the American public, and business leaders, about retirement and retirement income — problems, perceptions, expectations and intentions.

Accordingly, we commissioned Louis Harris and Associates, Inc. to conduct a nation-wide survey of American employees, retirees and business leaders to determine these attitudes.

From the beginning of this project we allowed Louis Harris and Associates a completely free hand in the development of the methodology and in the analysis and interpretation of the results. Our input was limited to advice and assistance in designing the survey and drafting the questionnaires, and in the funding of the project. All observations and conclusions that appear on the succeeding pages are those of the Harris organization and do not necessarily reflect the views of Johnson & Higgins. We will make our own comments separate and apart from this report.

Major findings having far-reaching implications emerged in these areas:

- Inflation and the quality of retired life

- Mandatory retirement changes

- Attitudes toward private pensions

- Attitudes toward Social Security

In some cases the results are about as expected. But in other cases the results are quite surprising!

This comprehensive survey is unique and most timely. The finding are extensive and should be of major significance to the American public — and, in particular, to governmental policymakers, business leaders, money managers, consultants, actuaries and other professionals who share more fully the responsibility for making the American retirement system work.

Johnson & Higgins is proud to present the result of this landmark survey.

Johnson & Higgins

TABLE OF CONTENTS

INDEX OF TABLES

CHAPTER IV: AN ASSESSMENT OF CURRENT SOURCES OF RETIREMENT INCOME

CHAPTER VII: PRIVATE PENSIONS: SOME POLICY CONSIDERATIONS

CHAPTER X: AN EMPLOYEE AND LEADERSHIP ASSESSMENT
OF SOCIAL SECURITY

CHAPTER XI: PUBLIC PENSIONS: SOME POLICY
CONSIDERATIONS

INTRODUCTION

Retirement and Income is a major study of employee, retiree and business leader attitudes toward pensions and the retirement income system in the United States.

In spite of the considerable amount of commentary and public attention it has engendered in the recent past, the issue of retirement and its financial implications is surrounded by as much confusion and uncertainty as ever before. The effects of ERISA, changes in the mandatory retirement law, impending major population shifts, inflation, and the prospect of further pension legislation — all these are contributing to the atmosphere of confusion and creating difficulty for the public and providers of retirement income alike. **Retirement and Income** has been commissioned by Johnson & Higgins in hopes of reducing some of the uncertainty which surrounds the retirement income system. The survey findings reported in these pages contain a wealth of reliable information, which, it is hoped, will be both illuminating and useful to policy makers, businessmen, and all those with an interest in the retirement income system in the United States.

Readers will be both consoled and concerned by the findings reported here. The survey brings a clear perspective to many issues confronting the private pension system. Many criticisms of private pensions conveyed by the media are not shared by business leaders or their employees, and both groups have much to say that is positive about pension legislation currently being considered. But some of the results are troubling. Many conventional assumptions are called into question, and the findings point to a number of potentially serious difficulties awaiting retirees and the providers of retirement income in the years ahead.

Above all, the results will set the record straight on attitudes toward retirement and pensions. They cast a much-needed light on the actions, attitudes, and concerns of employees regarding pensions and retirement. They bring into focus the difficulties faced by today's retirees, and suggest several ways the problems might be avoided in the future. Equally important, at a time when Congress is considering major changes in the pension laws, the findings provide a sharp portrait of the business community's attitudes toward ERISA and their concerns about the future of private pensions.

The survey is based on interviews with two separate samples: a national cross-section of 1699 current and retired employees, and a representative cross-section of 212 companies drawn from the Fortune listing and the *Dun and Bradstreet Million Dollar Directory.* The survey of employees consisted of 1330 interviews with full-time employees, and 369 interviews with people retired from full-time work. The focus of the study is on current and retired employees, rather than the entire adult public, because the former are primary contributors and beneficiaries of the Social Security System, and because they form that portion of the public most affected by pension legislation. For the sample of companies, interviews were conducted with corporate executives designated by their chief executive to speak on behalf of their company about pensions and retirement. All the fieldwork was conducted in August 1978. Details of the sample and methodology are given in the Appendix.

Louis Harris and Associates is grateful for the advice and assistance provided by Johnson & Higgins in designing the survey and drafting the questionnaires. However, the final responsibility for the design and implementation of the survey rests with the Harris firm.

It does not necessarily follow that Johnson & Higgins agrees or disagrees with any of the answers given by the employee or leadership groups, or with any of the observations or comments made in this report.

It should be noted that percentages in the tables may not always total 100%, because of rounding or the acceptance of multiple responses.

OVERVIEW AND SUMMARY OF MAJOR FINDINGS

From among the hundreds of results emerging from these surveys of employees, retirees, and business leaders, four sets of major findings have particularly important and far-reaching implications for the retirement and retirement income policies of government and business:

    I. Inflation and the Quality of Retired Life;
    II. Mandatory Retirement;
    III. Attitudes Toward Private Pensions;
    IV. Attitudes Toward Social Security.

The following is an overview and summary of these sets of major findings. Readers should be forewarned that many of the details and nuances of the results are unavoidably lost when summarizing a study of this size. Those whose interest is spurred by the findings below are urged to examine the full report.

I. INFLATION AND THE QUALITY OF RETIRED LIFE

Perhaps the most striking finding in this survey of business leaders and current and retired employees is the pervasive impact of inflation on attitudes toward pensions and retirement income expectations. The rapidly rising cost of living is imposing severe financial difficulties on sizeable proportions of today's retirees, particularly on those who do not receive pension benefits. More than 4 of every 10 retirees, and more than 5 of every 10 retirees who do not receive pension benefits claim that inflation has seriously reduced their standard of living. Current employees are also feeling the impact of inflation, which is limiting their ability to save for retirement while increasing the amount of money they believe they will need during retirement.

Having far-reaching consequences for the providers of retirement income, the pressures of inflation are boosting retirement income needs and expectations. The survey findings, coupled with projections of demographic shifts which will significantly increase the number of employees reaching retirement age beginning in the 1980's, suggest that today's employees are likely to exert considerable pressure for higher benefits from business and government as they approach retirement.

At the same time, however, the findings show that part of the solution to future increases in pension costs may lie with employees themselves. Employees are willing to make contributions to their company pension plans if their contributions can be made in exchange for larger benefits or earlier benefit eligibility. More than two-thirds of the employees interviewed say they would be willing to contribute to a plan, or to contribute more than they do now, if it would increase their retirement benefits. More than anything, employees would be willing to increase their contributions if their plan would provide benefits that increase with the cost of living (74-16% willing). Certainly these findings must be approached with some caution, since the difference between what people will actually accept and what they say they will accept can be considerable. However, at the very least, the findings demonstrate that increased employee contributions in exchange for earlier or larger benefits may provide a way to ease the burden of future retirement income demands.

Below, in summary form, are the major survey findings about inflation and its impact on retirement income expectations and the quality of retired life:

A. Inflation is clearly the number one problem facing retirees and the providers of retirement income today. Retirees have been the hardest hit by inflation, particularly retirees who are not receiving pension benefits. More than 4 of 10 retired employees say that inflation has seriously reduced their standard of living, and roughly another 4 in 10 say it has reduced their standard of living to some degree. Among those not receiving pension benefits, a full 53% say inflation has seriously reduced their standard of living compared with a smaller 28% holding the same view among pensioners.

Business leaders are also feeling the pressures of inflation. When asked about the disadvantages of pension plans to their company, a sizeable 61% cite increasing costs in an inflationary economy as the main disadvantage.

The government and government spending (Federal, Congressional, state and local) are among the major causes of inflation today according to current and retired employees and business leaders.

B. **A majority of retirees are satisfied with the quality of retired life, but for many, retirement is a time of financial hardship.** Sixty-five percent of those who are currently retired from full-time work believe the quality of retired life is at least as good as the quality of working life. However, 34% feel the quality of retired life is worse than the quality of working life, and nearly two-thirds of the retirees in this group say that financial problems are at the root of their dissatisfaction.

Over half (58%) of those retired from full-time jobs feel that their current standard of living is at least adequate, but a sizeable 42% feel that their income provides a standard of living which is less than adequate. Having a pension clearly makes a difference in a person's standard of living during retirement. More than half of those (56%) who do not receive pension benefits but just 23% of those who receive pension benefits believe that their current income provides a less than adequate standard of living.

The findings further suggest that many retirees are not able to afford some of life's basic necessities. In response to a question in which retirees were asked what they would do if they had an additional $100 a month, small but significant percentages report that they would buy food (18%), buy clothes (12%), pay off old debts (14%), or go to a doctor or dentist (7%).

C. **Spurred by inflation, retirement income expectations are rising, and the providers of retirement income are likely to feel increasing pressure for larger benefits in the years ahead.** To current and retired employees, by far the most important of several possible characteristics of pension plans (i.e., guaranteed benefits, portability, vesting, etc.) is that the plan have benefits that go up with the cost of living. A significant 66% list this pension plan characteristic as extremely important, and another 27% call it very important.

D. **Though many retirees are dissatisfied with their standard of living, overwhelming majorities of employees and business leaders feel the standard of living during retirement should be about the same as it was before retirement** — a goal which may lead to increased demands for higher and more liberal benefits as inflation continues to erode retirement incomes. Eighty-one percent of current employees and 84% of retirees feel that the standard of living during retirement should be about the same as before retirement; only 8% of each group think the standard of living during retirement should be higher than before retirement. This is in dramatic contrast to the 42% of retirees that feel that their income provides a standard of living which is less than adequate. And while nearly 2 out of 10 business leaders think retirement income should be less than pre-retirement income, a high 82% feel it should be about the same as before retirement.

E. **Employees are willing to contribute to their pension plans, or to contribute more than they do now, in exchange for various types of additional pension benefits.**

Sixty-eight percent of the employees interviewed would be willing to increase their contributions if it increased their retirement benefits. Employees say they would be most willing to increase their contributions to their pension plan if the plan provided benefits that increased with inflation and the cost of living (74-16% willing). By smaller margins, employees say they would be willing to increase contributions if their plan let them become eligible to receive benefits at an earlier age (61-27%), if the plan had a 100% guarantee that they would receive pension benefits regardless of investment performance (60-29%), and if the plan provided survivor's benefits to their spouse (58-31%).

II. MANDATORY RETIREMENT

Though the survey findings point to mounting financial pressures on retirees and the providers of retirement income in the years ahead, they also reveal a trend that, in the long run, may significantly lessen the pressure on retirement benefit costs. Stemming from a number of economic and demographic trends as well as the recent change in the mandatory retirement law, the current trend toward early retirement may be reversed in the not-too-distant future. More than half of today's employees would prefer to continue working — either full-time or part-time, at the same job or a less demanding job — instead of retiring, and just less than half say they actually plan to continue working and defer retirement. Also, workers between 18 and 49 years of age are significantly less likely to look forward to retiring than older workers. This may be a perception that will change as workers grow older, but it also may point to an increasing preference for deferred retirement as the work force ages.

A. Pushing back the mandatory retirement age from 65 to 70 is welcomed by both current and retired employees and the business community, but only total abolition of mandatory retirement will satisfy public opinion. A large majority of current and retired employees and a smaller but still substantial majority of business leaders are firmly opposed to any mandatory retirement age whatsoever. By 88-10%, current employees believe that "nobody should be forced to retire because of age, if he wants to continue working and can still do a good job." The same view is held by 2 of every 3 (67%) business executives interviewed.

B. While a majority of employees look forward to retirement, significant percentages would prefer to work — either full-time or part-time, at the same job or a less demanding job — as an alternative to retirement. More than 1 in 4 (26%) employees would prefer to retire when they reach the normal retirement age for their employment. Another 22% would like to retire before they reach the normal retirement age for their employment. However, a total of 51% say they would prefer to continue with some type of employment.

Though older workers are more likely to say they look forward to retirement than younger workers, there is little difference between the two groups in actual retirement intentions. Roughly half (48%) of those between the ages of 50 and 64 say they intend to continue working instead of retiring, as do an almost equal percentage of younger workers. Among workers between 50 and 64, 95% are covered by Social Security, 62% are covered by a private pension plan, and 28% are covered by a government employee plan.

C. A substantial percentage of today's retirees voice a strong desire to work during or instead of retirement. Nearly half (46%) of today's retirees would prefer to be working, while an even half (50%) would not. Not only would significant numbers of retired people prefer to work, but more than half would have preferred to continue working instead of retiring. Assuming they had an adequate retirement income, 31% of current retirees would have preferred to retire when they reached the normal retirement age. Another 12% would have preferred to retire before they reached the normal retirement age. The remaining 53% would have preferred to continue in some kind of employment.

III. ATTITUDES TOWARD PRIVATE PENSIONS

Both before and after the Employee Retirement Income Security Act of 1974, private pension plans have been criticized for being financially unsound, for promising what they may not be able to deliver, and for various inequities in the way employees become eligible for benefits. Whatever the possible merits of these criticisms, they are not, for the most part, fully shared by people currently covered by private pension plans. Most employees (78%) claim to be basically satisfied with the way their plans are designed and administered. And while approximately 1 in 3 (31%) express less than full confidence in their plans, a 68% majority have a great deal of confidence that their plans will pay the benefits to which they are entitled upon retirement. Of those who are not fully confident, only 6% have no confidence at all in their plans.

At the same time, these positive attitudes cannot be interpreted as public acceptance of the status quo in the private pension system. While employees say they are satisfied with plan design and administration, many place a high priority on types of provisions which are not found in most private plans today. Foremost among these are cost of living benefits, which are likely to become an increasingly central focus of employee demands if high levels of inflation persist, benefits which will permit the same standard of living as before retirement and survivor benefits.

The Employee Retirement Income Security Act has brought substantial changes in the types and amounts of information about pensions given to employees. The survey findings show that receiving information about their pension plan is extremely important to employees, but employees and employers have widely divergent views as to the types of information that should be reported. Employees place a higher priority than employers think necessary on receiving information about the current financial status of their pension plans in areas such as where funds are being invested, who is managing the funds, and the return on investment. However, it should be noted that employees are generally satisfied with the information they currently receive, and majorities say they find the reports they receive from their employers understandable and helpful. While the contents of reports may be improved, the limiting factor in employee knowledge about pension plans is not the reports themselves but that many employees fail to read them.

In the final analysis, having a pension plan at work is extremely important to today's employees. While employers and employees are not without criticisms of private plans, if anything, the findings suggest that both groups would favor an expansion of the private pension system:

A. Having a pension plan is a high priority among current employees. By 80-16%, employees feel that *"every employer should be required by law to provide a reasonable pension plan for his employees."* Employers have generally favorable attitudes toward pension plans and see many advantages in them for their company. However, they disagree that they should be required by law to provide such plans by 67-33%.

B. Employees covered by private plans voice relatively high levels of satisfaction with the way their plans are designed and administered, and a majority (68%) have a great deal of confidence that their plans will pay them the benefits to which they are entitled when they retire. Seventy-eight percent of those covered by private plans are at least somewhat satisfied with the way their plans are designed and administered, while 16% are at least somewhat dissatisfied. Although a commendable two-thirds of private plan participants have a great deal of confidence in their plan's ability to deliver, 25% are less than fully confident. Six percent have no confidence in their plan at all.

C. Private pension plans get generally high ratings from business leaders when compared with plans for government employees, union plans, and Social Security. Current and retired employees are mildly positive about private plans, but they are most positive about plans for government employees. Similar to business leaders, current and retired employees are most negative about union plans and Social Security. Business leaders, not surprisingly, are most positive about private plans, believing them to offer the highest benefits for the money contributed, and to be the best run. Business leaders are highly negative in their views toward union plans and Social Security, claiming that they are the sources of retirement income most in need of change.

A plurality (33%) of current and retired employees feel that plans for government employees offer the highest benefits for the money contributed and (by a 36% plurality) would prefer this type of plan over all others if they had to rely on only one plan for all their retirement income. Like business leaders, current and retired employees hold generally negative views of union plans and Social Security.

D. While employees say they are generally satisfied with plan design and administration, many place a high priority on types of provisions which are not found in most private plans today. By far the most important feature to have in a pension plan, according to current and retired employees, is a provision for benefits which increase with the cost of living. A striking 93% list this characteristic as at least very important. Sizeable majorities also feel it is at minimum "very important" to have guaranteed benefits regardless of investment performance, and to have survivor benefits. Business leaders consider cost of living benefits to be much less important than do current and retired employees. Instead, they feel it is most important that employees be guaranteed benefits regardless of investment performance, and that employees be guaranteed to receive vested benefits if they leave the job before retirement. Business leaders share the views of employees about the importance of having a provision for survivor benefits in pension plans.

E. Many employees, retirees, and employers would favor changes in the pension law to permit tax deductible employee contributions. Nearly half (49%) of the working and retired public would favor a change in the pension law which would permit employees to contribute to pension plans at work and deduct their contributions from federal taxes until they retire, while 28% would disapprove of the change. The proposal receives strong support in the business community, where 89% say they would approve of a law permitting tax-deductible employee contributions to pension plans at work.

Employees and employers would also welcome a law permitting the establishment of tax deductible IRAs along with participation in an employer pension plan.

F. While a majority of employees say they would be willing to contribute to their pension plan, most employers do not think they should be required to do so. Just 26% of the leaders interviewed say employees should be required to contribute to their pension plan and 72% say they should not.

G. Though employees are relatively satisfied with the pension information they currently receive, business leaders widely misjudge the importance employees place on certain types of information about their pension plans. Among employees who read their most recent pension report, substantial majorities believe it is "very important" that they receive information about the current financial status of their plan (83%), where pension funds are being invested (60%), who is managing pension funds (60%), and the return on investment (59%). However, among business leaders whose employees receive annual reports, just 38% feel it is "very important" that the report contain information about the current financial status of the plan, and less than 20% believe it is important to include information about who is managing the funds, where the funds are invested, and the return on investment. Nonetheless, majorities of those who have read their last pension report rate it positively for the information provided.

H. Many private pension plan participants are familiar with some of the basic provisions of their plan, but the results show that there is ample room for improvement in their knowledge. Most seem to know whether or not they are vested, though substantial minorities were uncertain or incorrect about vesting criteria. Also, more than half are uncertain about the size of their monthly retirement benefit. Even among those who are relatively close to retirement (50 to 64 years old), 58% do not know the approximate size of their monthly retirement benefit.

I. Portability: employees have mixed views as to how their pension benefits should be handled if they change jobs before retirement. A narrow 34% plurality feel that their accrued benefits should be kept in their original pension plan and the benefits paid out when they retire. Thirty-one percent would prefer that the money be transferred to a separate account of their own, like an IRA, and paid to them when they retire, while an almost equal 29% would prefer that the money be transferred to their new pension plan. Only 2% of employees covered by a pension plan and 1% of business leaders would prefer that the money be transferred to the federal government until retirement.

J. Integrated benefit formulas, by which the amount a person will receive from Social Security is taken into account when determining the size of his pension benefits, are met with opposing views by business leaders and current and retired employees. By 77-22%, a majority of business leaders feel that Social Security benefits should be taken into account when determining the size of a pension benefit. But by 55-37%, a majority of current and retired employees believe that Social Security benefits should not be taken into account.

IV. ATTITUDES TOWARD SOCIAL SECURITY

A large majority of today's work force expects to receive income from Social Security when they retire. Yet substantial numbers, particularly among younger employees, have little confidence in Social Security's ability to pay their retirement benefits. More than 8 out of 10 current employees have less than full confidence that Social Security will pay them benefits to which they are entitled when they retire; 42% have "hardly any confidence at all."

The findings suggest increased political pressure on Social Security in the future, much of which may be in the form of an increased demand to use general revenues or other revenue sources to fund Social Security. A majority of current and retired employees generally agree that, if necessary, more money should be collected from working people so the income of retirees can keep up with inflation. This, coupled with the growing numbers of employees who will be retiring in the years ahead, suggests an upward demand and increasing political pressure for larger Social Security benefits and, consequently, higher Social Security taxes. Moreover, while 45% of current and retired employees feel that Social Security benefits should be paid out of Social Security taxes, 47% feel that at least part of the money should come from other taxes.

Employees and retirees want the Social Security System to work, and most (76%) want it to work as was originally intended — a program to provide a basic level of retirement income that will supplement other retirement income sources. What is needed, the findings suggest, are ways to restore the public's confidence in the Social Security System.

A. **The vast majority of the working public are relying on Social Security for income during retirement, yet many are skeptical about the system's ability to pay out future retirement benefits.** Eighty-seven percent of today's employees expect to receive benefits from Social Security when they retire. However, more than 4 out of 5 employees have less than full confidence that Social Security will be able to pay the benefits owed them when they retire, and more than 2 out of 5 have hardly any confidence at all. Moreover, employees list Social Security over government employee plans, private plans and union plans as the source of retirement income most in need of a change for the better.

B. **Current and retired employees feel strongly that Social Security benefits should be increased with the cost of living, as is done now, but they have mixed views as to what moneys should be used to provide benefits to current and future retirees.** Eighty-six percent of current and retired employees feel that Social Security benefits should increase at least as fast as the cost of living over the next five years, while only 9% believe they should be kept the same. With a view sharply divergent to that of business leaders, a narrow plurality (47%) of current employees and retirees feel that at least part of the money for Social Security benefits should come from sources other than Social Security taxes: 42% feel that part should come from other taxes, and 5% that *all* benefits should come from other taxes. By 79-20%, business leaders feel all Social Security benefits should be paid from Social Security taxes.

C. **A 76% majority of current and retired employees believe that Social Security should provide a basic level of retirement income, while 17% believe it should provide all retirement income.** Among those who feel Social Security should provide a basic level of retirement income, 22% believe it should provide a basic level of income regardless of pre-retirement income and 31% believe that it should provide a basic level of income while taking previous income into account. Another 23% feel Social Security should provide a basic level of income which should be used as a supplement to other retirement income. Part of the reason for low interest among current and retired employees in having all retirement income provided through Social Security is a lack of confidence in the government's ability to manage such a program. Nearly half the respondents (49%) have hardly any confidence in the government's ability to run a program in which all retirement income would be distributed through the federal government and funded by taxes.

ADDITIONAL FINDINGS

BUSINESS ATTITUDES TOWARD ERISA

1. **Business leaders have mixed views on ERISA: in general, they rate the law negatively, yet they hold strongly positive views toward a number of the law's basic provisions. Negative business attitudes toward ERISA stem primarily from the time, paperwork, and costs required to administer a plan.** Many of the major criticisms frequently heard about ERISA, such as its effect on investment performance, fiduciary standards, and pension eligibility requirements, are not shared by the sizeable percentages of the country's business leaders who are involved with company pensions. ERISA's fiduciary standards, for instance, receive a 76-21% positive rating from business leaders. The law's vesting requirements are rated positively by 90-10%. Also viewed favorably are ERISA's pension eligibility requirements (78-20%), joint and survivor benefit regulations (87-10%), funding standards (76-16%) and plan termination insurance (58-36%).

Overall, however, businessmen give the law a 61-38% negative rating. The reason for this rating lies primarily with the law's reporting and disclosure requirements, and the cost, paperwork, and executive time which they engender. ERISA's reporting and disclosure requirements meet a strong 71-28% disapproval among business leaders. By 57-34% leaders say ERISA has a negative impact on the time it takes executives to deal with pension matters. And the law is thought to have had a negative impact on a company's cost of having a pension plan, by 54-30%.

2. **A full 69% of the leaders interviewed feel that ERISA has had little or no effect on the basic investment strategy for their company's pension fund.** Another 14% claim that the funding and fiduciary requirements of ERISA have resulted in different, but not necessarily more conservative, investment strategies for pension funds. Just 15% charge that ERISA's funding and fiduciary requirements have resulted in more conservative investment strategies for their company.

BUSINESS ATTITUDES TOWARD PENSION FUNDING AND UNFUNDED LIABILITIES

1. **Most business leaders feel their company's pension plan is at least adequately funded.** In terms of the benefits that have been promised, 69% claim their company's plan is well-funded, 29% claim it is adequately funded, and only 2% say their plan is under-funded. Generally, the larger the percentage of vested liabilities which are unfunded, the less positive business leaders are about the adequacy of their plan's funding.

2. **Fifty-six percent of the companies in the sample have some portion of their vested pension liabilities which is unfunded and 44% do not.** Thirty-four percent of the firms have unfunded vested liabilities amounting to 25% or less of their total vested liabilities, 17% have unfunded vested liabilities of between 26% and 50% of total vested liabilities, and 4% have unfunded vested liabilities which account for more than half of their total vested liabilities.

3. **Business leaders are considerably concerned about the problem of unfunded pension liabilities, but they are generally not alarmed.** Many feel that the problem has been overblown, and that liabilities will be reduced by better investment results and amortization over a number of years. Still, a small but substantial minority are deeply concerned about the problem. Sixteen percent say unfunded pension liabilities are a major concern to their company, and a further 38% say they are a minor concern.

4. By 66-19%, business leaders feel pension funds should be invested wherever they bring the largest return, regardless of the social policies of the companies or countries in which they might be invested. Employees covered by private pensions are nearly evenly split on the issue, with a narrow plurality favoring investing funds wherever they bring the largest return if following socially desirable investment policies meant retirees would receive lower pension benefits. It should be noted that a substantial minority feel strongly that funds should not be invested in companies or countries with socially undesirable policies.

PRE-RETIREMENT PLANNING

1. The experience of today's retirees shows that pre-retirement planning is critical to a secure retirement: current retirees who had inadequately planned for their retirement are considerably more likely than others to have an inadequate amount of retirement income. Among those who feel they had done enough planning, for instance, 10% claim their income is less than adequate. But the same claim is made by 56% of the retirees who say they had done far too little or no planning at all.

2. Sizeable percentages of today's employees feel they have done little planning and made few preparations for their retirement. This is true for older as well as younger employees. Thirty percent of current employees have done no planning at all for their retirement, as have a smaller but substantial 20% of those between the ages of 50 and 64. Forty-eight percent of employees between 50 and 64 years of age (and 58% among all employees) have not given any thought to how much money they will need when they finally retire. More than 1 in 5 of these older employees intend to retire without a pension.

GOVERNMENT EMPLOYEE PENSION PLANS

Strong majorities of current and retired employees and of business leaders feel that public pension plans should be subject to the same regulations for funding, reporting, and eligibility requirements as are private pensions. Public plan compliance with private plan regulations is favored by 68% of current and retired employees (14% opposed), and by an overwhelming 93% of business leaders. Moreover, such compliance is favored by a sizeable 65% majority of employees currently covered by public plans and opposed by only 18%.

DOUBLE DIPPING

There is only mild public opposition to the practice of double dipping. By 51-42%, a narrow majority of current and retired employees believe that people who retire after 20 years of service on a government job should be able to collect a government pension while working at a second job. Business leaders take an opposite view, believing by 50-30% that retired government workers should not be able to collect a government pension while working at a second job. Lastly, both current employees and retirees as well as business leaders feel that people who retire after 20 years of government service and who then work and retire from a second job should be able to collect two pensions — one for each job they have had.

CHAPTER I:

INFLATION AND THE QUALITY OF RETIRED LIFE

The Quality of Retired Life

A majority of retirees enjoy at least the same or a higher quality of life during retirement as when they were working. But for millions, retirement brings a decline in the quality of life.

When asked to compare the quality of retirement life with the quality of working life, 41% of retirees in the sample say that retirement life is better and 24% say it is about the same, but a high 34% — more than 1 of every 3 interviewed — claim that the quality of retired life is worse than the quality of working life. This translates into over 8 million Americans who are less than satisfied with the quality of their retirement life.

The way people feel about retired life is clearly linked to whether or not they are receiving pension benefits, with pensioners holding generally more positive views. Among those currently receiving pensions, 41% feel that life now is better than when they were working, 29% feel it is about the same, and 30% feel their lives now are worse than when they were working. Among those not receiving pension benefits, 37% feel retired life is worse than working life, while 22% think it is about the same and 39% think it is better.

Table I-1

QUALITY OF RETIRED LIFE COMPARED TO QUALITY OF WORKING LIFE
(Asked of retired employees)

Q.: First I'd like to ask you some questions about retirement. Overall, how would you say the quality of retired life compares with life when you were working — is it much better, somewhat better, about the same, somewhat worse, or much worse than when you were working?

(Number of respondents)	Total (397)	Receiving Pension Benefits (294)	Not Receiving Pension Benefits (93)
	%	%	%
Much better	22	28	15
Somewhat better	19	13	24
About the same	24	29	22
Somewhat worse	19	20	18
Much worse	15	10	19
Not sure	1	1	1

Among those who are satisfied with retired life, many cite the freedom of retirement life, a more relaxed lifestyle, and more recreation time as reasons that retired life is better than working life. Twenty percent say they enjoy retired life more because they can do as they please and have no schedule to meet, 15% because they can take it easier and have no worries, and 10% because they have more time for recreation and socializing. In addition, 7% enjoy having more time for family and friends.

Why is the quality of retired life worse than that of working life for so many retirees? More than anything else, retirees are hampered by financial problems. The financial problems inherent in fixed retirement incomes are mentioned by 21% of retirees, far more than mention any other single problem. Closely related to this are problems caused by inflation and the high cost of living, cited by 7%.

Additionally, 9% of retirees say they don't feel active or useful, 7% feel their time was better occupied when they were working, 7% mention health problems, and 6% simply prefer to work. Three percent are dissatisfied with the quality of retired life because they are lonely.

Again, whether or not they receive pension benefits has a significant effect on the way people perceive the quality of their retired life. While 28% of those who are not receiving benefits say they are worse off because of financial problems, only 11% of those receiving pension benefits make the same claim. Similarly, inflation, excess time, and health seem to be less problematic for people receiving pension benefits than for those not receiving them.

Table I-2

WHY RETIRED LIFE IS BETTER OR WORSE THAN WORKING LIFE
(Asked of those who find retired life better or worse than working life)

Q.: Why do you feel that way? Any other reason?

(Number of respondents)	Total Retirees (397)	Receiving Pension Benefits (294)	Not Receiving Pension Benefits (93)
	%	%	%
Worse	*34*	*30*	*37*
Financially worse off, don't have as much money, fixed income	21	11	28
Don't feel active and useful, no commitment to anything, nothing to look forward to	9	11	8
Inflation, rising prices, high cost of living	7	5	9
Time better occupied when working, excess time wasted	7	5	9
Health reasons, don't feel well	7	5	8
Prefer working	6	4	8
I'm alone/lonesome	3	5	1
Forced to retire, involuntary retirement	2	1	2
Better	*41*	*41*	*39*
Can do as I please when I please, no schedule to meet, get away from routine	20	21	20
Take it easier, don't have to push, no worries	15	10	17
More recreation time, more socializing, more reading, T.V., etc.	10	14	7
More time for family and friends	7	7	6
I enjoy retirement, my retirement is good	4	5	3
Financially better off, stable, live better today	3	4	2
More time	1	2	—
I'm self employed now/my own boss	1	2	—
I'm in good health	*	1	—
Any other answer	6	4	6
Not sure	—	—	—

*Less than 0.5%.

2

The primary reason for the high levels of dissatisfaction with retirement life can be seen more clearly in Table I-3. While more than half of the retirees interviewed (58%) feel that their current income provides at least an adequate standard of living, a sizeable 42% feel that their current income permits a less than adequate standard of living.

Again, the adequacy of a person's standard of living during retirement is linked to whether or not he receives pension benefits. Seventy-six percent of those receiving benefits, but only 43% of those who do not receive benefits, feel that their present income provides at least an adequate standard of living. And it comes as no surprise that a large 56% of those who do not receive pension benefits feel their standard of living is less than adequate, compared with 23% among pensioners who hold the same view.

Observation:

These findings should dispel the notion that the years spent in retirement are the "golden years" of one's life. While a majority of current retirees feel that their standard of living is adequate, and many are satisfied with the quality of retired life, an alarming number of people are dissatisfied and existing on what they feel is an inadequate standard of living.

For two reasons, these findings are an early warning of potential trouble ahead for government, for business, and for retirees themselves. First, most experts agree that the increasing pressures of inflation and the rising cost of living are not about to subside. Unless some relief is found, retired workers may well be worse off in the future than they are today. Second, the number of retired workers is likely to increase significantly in the near future, partly because of demographic shifts in the population, and partly because of a short-term trend toward earlier retirement (see Chapter II). As retirees grow in number and become more politically powerful, and as inflation continues to eat into their spending power, retirees are likely to exert considerable pressure on business and government for increases in their retirement income. Some of the possible effects of this problem, along with several ways they might be avoided, are suggested in many of the findings discussed in later chapters.

Table I-3

ADEQUACY OF STANDARD OF LIVING AMONG RETIREES
(Asked of retired employees)

Q.: Overall, does your present income provide you with a more than adequate standard of living, an adequate standard of living or a less than adequate standard of living?

(Number of respondents)	Total (396)	Receiving Pension Benefits (297)	Not Receiving Pension Benefits (96)
	%	%	%
More than adequate	12	16	8
Adequate	46	60	35
Less than adequate	42	23	56
Not sure	*	1	—

*Less than 0.5%.

The Impact of Inflation

Early evidence of the impact of inflation on retirement income expectations can already be seen in the survey findings. For instance, adding provisions to pension plans that would keep benefits in line with inflation is easily the working public's most important concern when it comes to pension plan design. When presented with a number of features that might be included in a pension plan, such as benefits permitting a pre-retirement standard of living, survivors' benefits, vesting privileges, portability, and pension benefit guarantees, the bulk of employees (58%) select "that your pension benefits will go up as the cost of living goes up" as the most important feature to have in their pension plan. This is followed, not surprisingly, by 46% who feel the most important feature in a plan is that it provide enough money for them to maintain the same standard of living as before their retirement (see Chapter VII).

As seen in Table I-4, overwhelming majorities of current and retired employees and of business leaders feel the standard of living during retirement should be about the same as it was before retirement. Eighty-one percent of current employees and 84% of retirees feel that the standard of living during retirement should be about the same as before retirement; only 8% of each group think the standard of living during retirement should be higher than before retirement. And while nearly 2 out of 10 business leaders think retirement income should be less than pre-retirement income, a high 82% feel it should be about the same as before retirement.

Observation:

In part, current employees' hopes of maintaining a pre-retirement standard of living into retirement stems from an obvious and understandable reluctance to give up the comfort and convenience they have grown accustomed to during their working lives. But their concern about their post-retirement standard of living is also fueled by a fear of inflation. As will be seen in later findings, this fear of inflation and its impact on retirement is likely to result in demands for increases in the amounts and types of retirement benefits.

Employees may be unrealistic in their hopes of maintaining a pre-retirement standard of living after retirement, since most people's standard of living drops when they leave work. But this will not prevent them from increasing demands on the providers of retirement income. By seeking an income which will provide the same standard of living as before retirement, employees may be hoping to minimize the effects of inflation on their post-retirement purchasing power. Employees' concern about the adequacy of their retirement income and their demands for increased pension and Social Security benefits are likely to be directly linked to business and government's ability to deal with inflation.

Table I-4

ATTITUDES TOWARD POST-RETIREMENT STANDARD OF LIVING
(Asked of current and retired employees and of business leaders)

Q.: When a person retires, do you think their standard of living should be higher than before they retired, lower than before, or about the same as it was before retirement?

(Number of respondents)	Total Current Employees (1328) %	Total Retired Employees (398) %	Total Business Leaders (212) %
Higher	8	8	—
Lower	9	7	18
About the same	81	84	82
Not sure	1	*	*

*Less than 0.5%.

Inflation has had a strong impact on people who are working as well as on retirees. Thirty-one percent of those who are employed claim that inflation seriously reduces their standard of living, and 57% claim it reduces it to some degree. Only 11% say that inflation has almost no effect at all.

Of course, the effect of inflation on standard of living is most severe among retirees, particularly among retirees who are not receiving pension benefits. A sizeable 53% of those who are not receiving pension benefits say that inflation seriously reduces their standard of living, while another 34% say it reduces it to some degree.

Significant percentages of people in all sectors of society feel the impact of inflation. However, nowhere is its impact more severe than on lower income groups. More than 1 of every 2 people (52%) earning under $7,000 a year say that inflation seriously reduces their standard of living, a sentiment echoed by 38% of those earning between $7,000 and $14,999, 29% of those earning between $15,000 and $24,999, and 20% of those earning $25,000 a year or more.

Table I-5

EFFECT OF INFLATION ON STANDARD OF LIVING
(Asked of current and retired employees)

Q.: Let's talk about inflation for a minute. What impact does inflation have on your standard of living — would you say it seriously reduces your standard of living to some degree, or does it have almost no effect at all on your standard of living?

(Number of respondents)	Total Current Employees (1324) %	Retired Employees Total (393) %	Retired Employees Receiving Pension Benefits (294) %	Retired Employees Not Receiving Pension Benefits (95) %	Current and Retired Employees Income Under $7,000 (234) %	Current and Retired Employees Income $7,000-$14,999 (532) %	Current and Retired Employees Income $15,000-$24,999 (554) %	Current and Retired Employees Income $25,000 And Over (310) %
Seriously reduces	31	42	28	53	52	38	29	20
Reduces to some degree	57	42	51	34	36	52	60	60
Almost no effect at all	11	15	20	10	10	9	10	19
Not sure	1	2	1	2	2	2	1	1

Lastly, the effect of inflation on retirees is further demonstrated in Table I-6, which reports the results of a question in which retirees were asked what they would do if they had an additional $100 a month. If they had an additional $100 a month, many retirees would buy necessities such as food, clothes, or health services. While it is true that the largest percentages of the total sample of retirees would save most or a large portion of the money (32%) or take a vacation (21%), sizeable proportions would stick to more basic needs: fixing up their house or apartment (21%), buying food (18%), buying clothes (12%), paying off old debts (14%), and going to a doctor or dentist (7%).

Perhaps most striking are the responses given by retirees who believe their standard of living is less than adequate; their choices of what to do with an additional $100 a month underline the sincerity of their claim. Number one on the list of things to do is to buy food, mentioned by 30% of the respondents in this group. A high 25% would pay off old debts, 24% would fix up their house or apartment, and 22% would buy clothes. More than 1 in 10 (14%) would use the money to see a doctor or dentist.

Observation:

Two important conclusions can be drawn from the survey findings up to this point. First, after a lifetime of work, many retirees find themselves in severe financial difficulties, because of both their own inadequate planning (as will be shown in a later section) and the pressures of inflation on a fixed income. Secondly, though not a panacea, having a pension makes a significant difference in the quality of one's retired life. Retirees who are currently receiving pension benefits are likely to be more satisfied with retired life than non-recipients, have a more adequate standard of living, and be less vulnerable to the impact of inflation. The experience of retirees with the needs of retirement living holds many important lessons for people who are currently working; these will be outlined in a later section.

Table I-6

WHERE RETIREES WOULD SPEND EXTRA INCOME
(Asked of retired employees)

Q.: Suppose your average monthly income were increased by $100. Which of the things on this list would you be most likely to do if you had an additional $100 a month?

(Number of respondents)	Total (390)	Standard Of Living		
		More Than Adequate (52)	Adequate (223)	Less Than Adequate (121)
	%	%	%	%
Save most or a large portion of the money	32	62	36	19
Take a trip or a vacation	21	16	30	15
Fix up your house or apartment	21	12	22	24
Buy food	18	2	12	30
Invest the money	14	38	19	1
Pay off old debts	14	—	7	25
Buy clothes	12	4	7	22
Go to a doctor or dentist	7	—	2	14
Buy a major appliance item, such as a refrigerator or air conditioner	4	2	6	3
Buy furniture	4	2	5	3
Buy a car	3	4	3	5
Move to a different or better place to live	3	—	2	5
Buy a major item for recreation or entertainment, such as a color television or a stereo	2	—	4	2
Other	6	—	6	7
Not sure	3	2	4	3

Fighting Inflation

The government and government spending, according to current and retired employees and business leaders, are among the major causes of inflation today. Sixty-three percent of current and retired employees say federal spending is a major cause of inflation today, 48% blame spending by Congress, and 37% look to state and local spending. Also high on the list of causes of inflation are food prices (50%), major oil companies (49%), increased health and medical costs (46%), welfare and relief payments (46%), union wage demands (44%), Arab oil-producing countries (39%), and price increases by middlemen (34%). Additionally, high numbers of people cite interest rates (31%), a lack of leadership (31%), worldwide inflation (28%), business raising prices (26%), business profits (21%), defense spending (21%), and shortages of resources and products such as gasoline and oil (19%) as major causes of inflation.

Business leaders are even more sharply focused on government and government policies as major causes of inflation today, with 98% — almost every business leader interviewed — citing federal spending as a major cause of inflation. Spending by Congress, state and local spending, welfare and relief payments, President Carter's economic policies — all these are mentioned by majorities of the leaders interviewed as major factors underlying the high rate of inflation. Also high on the businessmen's list are union wage demands (67%), Arab oil-producing countries (54%), a lack of leadership in the country (49%), increased health and medical costs (49%), and worldwide inflation (41%).

TABLE I-7

MAJOR CAUSES OF INFLATION
(Asked of current and retired employees and of business leaders)

Q.: Which items on this list would you say are major causes of inflation today?

(Number of respondents)	Total Current And Retired Employees (1695)	Total Business Leaders (212)
	%	%
Federal spending	63	98
Food prices	50	26
Major oil companies	49	13
Spending by Congress	48	81
Increased health and medical costs	46	49
Welfare and relief payments	46	55
Union wage demands	44	67
Arab oil-producing countries	39	54
State and local spending	37	71
Middleman price increases	34	23
High interest rates on borrowing money	31	14
Lack of leadership in the country	31	49
Worldwide inflation	28	41
Business raising prices	26	17
Business profits	21	4
Defense spending	21	25
Shortages of resources and products, such as gasoline and fuel oil	19	—
President Carter's economic policies	18	50
Spending by the public	12	10
Federal Reserve Board	10	10
Farm prices	10	11
Other	2	6
None	—	—
Not sure	1	—

Since many believe that the government is primarily responsible for inflation, sizeable percentages of current and retired employees and of business leaders feel that government should take a primary responsibility in solving the problem. When asked what steps they would be willing to accept to help control inflation, 64% of the current and retired employees interviewed say they would be very willing to accept less government spending and a reduction in government services. Of the various policies listed, this was by far the most acceptable. Similarly, 48% would be very willing to accept lower taxes and a reduction in government services. At the same time, sizeable percentages of current and retired employees feel that other sectors of society should share some of the burden for beating inflation. Half would be willing to accept tough government measures to keep business from raising prices, and 36% would be very willing to accept wage and price controls. Current and retired employees are strongly opposed to higher taxes (75% not willing to accept) and a higher rate of unemployment (60%).

Business leaders share employees' views on the government's responsibility in fighting inflation. Almost every businessman interviewed (97%) would be very willing to accept less government spending and a reduction in government services, and more than 3 out of 4 (76%) are very willing to accept lower taxes and a reduction in government services. Expectedly, majorities of businessmen are opposed to wage and price controls (75% not willing to accept), tough government measures to keep business from raising prices (59%) and higher taxes (59%). A higher rate of unemployment is more acceptable to businessmen than to current and retired employees, with 21% of the businessmen interviewed very willing, and 60% somewhat willing, to accept such a policy. Similarly, lower pay increases are more acceptable to businessmen, with 45% very willing and 47% somewhat willing to accept this condition.

TABLE I-8

WILLINGNESS TO ACCEPT VARIOUS CONDITIONS TO HELP CONTROL INFLATION
(Asked of current and retired employees)

Q.: In order to help control inflation would you be very willing, somewhat willing, or not at all willing to accept (ITEM)?

(Number of respondents: 1689)		Very Willing	Somewhat Willing	Not At All Willing	Not Sure
Less government spending and a reduction in government services	%	64	25	5	6
Tough government measure to keep business from raising prices	%	50	26	16	7
Lower taxes and a reduction in government services	%	48	32	9	10
Wage and price controls	%	36	30	24	10
Lower pay increases	%	21	41	31	8
A higher rate of unemployment	%	7	20	60	13
Higher taxes	%	4	16	75	5

TABLE I-9

EMPLOYERS' WILLINGNESS TO ACCEPT VARIOUS CONDITIONS TO HELP CONTROL INFLATION
(Asked of business leaders)

Q.: In order to help control inflation would you, as an employer, be very willing, somewhat willing, or not at all willing to accept (ITEM)?

(Number of respondents: 212)		Very Willing	Somewhat Willing	Not At All Willing	Not Sure
Less government spending and a reduction in government services	%	97	3	—	*
Lower taxes and a reduction in government services	%	76	20	2	2
Lower pay increases	%	45	47	6	2
A higher rate of unemployment	%	21	60	14	5
Tough government measures to keep business from raising prices	%	9	31	59	1
Wage and price controls	%	6	18	75	2

*Less than 0.5%.

Employee and Business Leader Willingness to Support Current Retirees

Although current employees and business leaders are opposed to higher taxes, they believe that money should be found — through taxes if necessary — to help current retirees keep up with inflation. In light of the impact of inflation on retirement incomes, and in spite of the fact that it would cost them more money, 56% of those currently employed full-time feel that more money should be collected from working people to help retirees keep up with inflation. Only 11% think that retirees should do the best they can on the pensions and Social Security benefits they get now. This view is echoed, though somewhat less strongly, by business leaders. .Forty-seven percent of the business leaders interviewed feel that collecting more money from working people to help retirees is the right thing to do, while 22% feel that retirees should do the best they can with what they have now.

Table I-10

WHETHER WORKING PEOPLE SHOULD CONTRIBUTE MORE TO HELP RETIREES KEEP UP WITH INFLATION
(Asked of current and retired employees and of business leaders)

Q.: Retired people who are on fixed incomes are hard hit by inflation these days. One of the ways of dealing with this problem has been to add cost-of-living provisions to Social Security and pension plans, so that the income of retirees can keep up with inflation. The problem with this is that the increased cost of pension and Social Security benefits will have to be made up by higher pension contributions and Social Security taxes from people who are working today. Which do you think is the right thing to do — to collect more money from people who are working so the incomes of retirees can keep up with inflation, or to let retirees do the best they can and to keep the pension and Social Security benefits of retirees the same as they are now?

(Number of respondents)	Current And Retired Employees			Total Business Leaders (210)
	Total (1688)	Current (1322)	Retired (394)	
	%	%	%	%
Collect more money from working people	54	56	49	47
Let retirees do the best they can	11	11	10	22
Both (vol.)	8	8	9	10
Neither (vol.)	16	15	18	18
Not sure	12	11	14	2

CHAPTER II:

ALTERNATIVES TO RETIREMENT

The costs to companies of having pension plans have soared in the past decade. Many factors have contributed to rising pension costs, chief among them being inflation, increased benefits, poor investment results and a trend toward early retirement. And, as seen in the previous chapter, the pressure on pension costs is likely to increase as greater proportions of workers reach retirement age, and inflation generates demands for higher benefits.

But the survey results reveal another trend that, in the long run, may significantly lessen the pressure on pension costs. Stemming from a number of economic and demographic trends as well as the recent change in the mandatory retirement law, the current tendency toward early retirement may be reversed in the not-too-distant future. As the results in this section demonstrate, there are already signs of change.

Attitudes Toward Mandatory Retirement

In January 1979, the age at which a worker may be forced to retire changed from 65 to 70. This change is welcomed by both current and retired employees and the business community, but evidence suggests that the change may not have gone far enough. A large majority of current and former employees, and a smaller but still substantial majority of business leaders, are firmly opposed to any mandatory retirement age whatsoever. By 88-10%, current employees believe that "nobody should be forced to retire because of age, if he wants to continue working and can still do a good job." The same view is held by 2 of every 3 (67%) business executives interviewed.

Thus the consensus among the working and retired public and business leaders is that as long as a person is productive he or she should be able to continue to work. But the two groups disagree on the productivity of older workers. By 64-33%, a majority of business executives disagree that "most older people can continue to perform as well on the job as they did when they were younger." Current employees hold the opposite view, with 57% agreeing and 37% disagreeing with the statement, as do retirees by 61-36%.

Neither current and retired employees nor business leaders are completely sold on the argument that deferred retirement will reduce employment and advancement opportunities for youth. The statement, "older people should be forced to retire at some age so as to open up jobs and promotions for young people," is opposed by majorities of current and retired employees, and by a narrow majority of business leaders.

Table II-1

ATTITUDES TOWARD VARIOUS STATEMENTS ON WORK AND RETIREMENT
(Asked of current and retired employees and of business leaders)

Q.: I'd like to read you some statements people have made about work and retirement. For each, please tell me whether you agree strongly, agree somewhat, disagree somewhat, or disagree strongly.

(Number of respondents)	Current Employees (1326)			Retired Employees (396)			Business Leaders (212)		
	Agree	Disagree	Not Sure	Agree	Disagree	Not Sure	Agree	Disagree	Not Sure
Nobody should be forced to retire because of age, if he wants to continue working and is still able to do a good job %	88	10	2	87	10	2	67	32	*
Most employers discriminate against older people and make it difficult for them to find work %	80	15	5	75	20	5	41	57	2
Older people should be forced to retire at some age so as to open up jobs and promotions for younger people %	34	62	4	37	55	8	46	53	1
Most older people can continue to perform as well on the job as they did when they were younger %	57	37	6	61	36	3	33	64	2

*Less than 0.5%.

Personal Outlooks on Retirement

Though many believe older people should not be forced to retire, a majority of employees (61%) think that most people look forward to retirement. Only 29% believe most people do not look forward to retiring.

Interestingly, however, this notion finds less support among younger workers. By a smaller margin of 52-39%, workers between 18 and 24 years of age believe most people look forward to retiring. But this attitude is held more strongly by workers between the ages of 50 and 64, by a sizeable 70-20%.

Table II-2

WHETHER MOST PEOPLE LOOK FORWARD TO RETIRING
(Asked of current employees)

Q.: Some people say that they look forward to not working; others say that they don't like the idea of not working at all. In general, how do you think most people feel about the idea of retiring — do you think they look forward to it, or not?

(Number of respondents)	Total (1319)	Age			
		18-24 (149)	25-34 (375)	35-49 (430)	50-64* (337)
	%	%	%	%	%
Look forward to retiring	61	52	55	62	70
Don't look forward to it	29	39	33	27	20
Not sure	11	9	12	12	9

*Regardless of whether or not they are covered by a pension, employees in this age group believe that most people look forward to retiring by a margin of approximately 70-20%.

When asked whether they personally look forward to retiring, a 54% majority of employees reply affirmatively. However, it should be noted that 2 out of every 5 workers say they do not look forward to retirement. A major factor in people's attitudes toward retirement is their type of employment. Hourly wage workers and salaried workers are more likely to look forward to retiring than those who are self-employed. Still, even among hourly wage workers and salaried workers, nearly 2 out of 5 do not look forward to retirement.

Again, there is a large difference in attitudes toward retirement among different age groupings, with younger workers being considerably less enthusiastic about retirement than older workers. While nearly 2 out of 3 workers between the ages of 50 and 64 look forward to retirement, a plurality (47-42%) of workers between the ages of 18 and 24 say they do not look forward to it.

Positive outlooks toward retirement are strongest among older workers covered by pension plans, particularly those covered by public plans. Sixty-three percent of private plan participants between 50 and 64 years of age look forward to retiring, as do 71% of those older workers covered by public plans. Among those between 50 and 64 years who are not covered by a pension, a smaller 58% look forward to retirement.

Interestingly, more people seem to be looking forward to retirement now than three years ago. When the same survey question was asked by Louis Harris and Associates for the National Council on Aging in 1974, 43% of the employees interviewed said they looked forward to retiring and 51% claimed they did not.

Observation:

The increase in positive attitudes toward retirement since 1974 is consistent with the well-documented trend toward early retirement. Given the opportunity to retire early with a substantial pension, many people look forward to retiring and are taking advantage of early retirement clauses in pension plans. However, attitudes among different age groupings — along with the findings discussed in the next section — suggest that this may not be the long-term trend.

Table II-3a

WHETHER PERSONALLY LOOK FORWARD TO RETIRING
(Asked of current employees)

Q.: Do you personally look forward to retiring, or not?

	1978								1974
	Employment			Age				
(Number of respondents)	Total (1309)	Hourly Wage Worker (534)	Salaried (584)	Self-Employed (159)	18-24 (148)	25-34 (372)	35-49 (426)	50-64 (336)	Total Employees (1332)
	%	%	%	%	%	%	%	%	%
Look forward to retiring	54	55	57	44	42	56	51	63	43
Don't look forward to it	40	38	38	52	47	40	42	33	51
Not sure	6	7	6	4	11	4	7	4	6

Table II-3b

WHETHER OLDER EMPLOYEES PERSONALLY LOOK FORWARD TO RETIRING
(Asked of current employees)

Q.: Do you personally look forward to retiring, or not?

(Number of respondents)	Employees Between 50 and 64			
	Total (336)	Pension Coverage		
		Private Plan (179)	Public Plan (75)	Not Covered (98)
	%	%	%	%
Look forward to retiring	63	64	71	58
Don't look forward to it	33	31	24	40
Not sure	4	5	4	3

Preferred Retirement Alternatives

While a majority of employees look forward to retirement, significant percentages would prefer to work — either full-time or part-time, at the same job or at a less demanding job — as an alternative to retirement.

Currently employed respondents were presented with a list of retirement alternatives and asked which one they would prefer to do. More than 1 in 4 (26%) would prefer to retire when they reach the normal retirement age for their employment. Another 22% would like to retire before they reach the normal retirement age for their employment. However, a total of 51% say they would prefer to continue with some type of employment:

- 8% would prefer to retire at a normal or early retirement age and take a job with another employer.
- 14% would prefer to continue working full-time at the same job at the same pay for as long as they can.
- 5% would prefer to work full-time as long as they can at a less demanding job with less pay.
- 24% would prefer to work part-time as long as they can.

Again, the type of employment — whether one is an hourly wage worker, a salaried worker or self-employed — is a major factor in attitudes toward retirement. The self-employed are more likely than either hourly wage workers or salaried workers to want to continue working as long as possible. In total, 71% of the self-employed would prefer to hold some type of job instead of retiring, compared with 53% of salaried workers and 42% of hourly wage workers who express the same view.

Table II-4

PREFERRED RETIREMENT AND/OR WORK ARRANGEMENT
(Asked of current employees)

Q.: Here is a list of things that people do about work when they get on in years. Assuming you would have an adequate amount of retirement income, which **one** of the things on this list would you prefer to do?

(Number of respondents)	Total (1322)	Hourly Wage Worker (540)	Salaried (594)	Self-Employed (160)
	%	%	%	%
Retire when I reach the normal retirement age for my employment	26	32	23	12
Retire before I reach the normal retirement age for my employment	22	24	23	13
Retire at a normal or early retirement age for my employment and take a job with another employer	8	6	12	3
Instead of retiring, continue to work full-time as long as I can at the same job and the same pay	14	14	13	16
Instead of retiring, continue to work full-time as long as I can at a less demanding job with less pay	5	5	4	6
Instead of retiring, continue to work part-time as long as I can	24	17	24	46
Other	1	1	1	2
Not sure	1	1	1	1

Table II-5 shows the age at which current workers would prefer to either retire or take some type of less demanding work. Among those who would prefer to retire at normal retirement age for their employment, the median age at which they would prefer to retire is 60.2 years. This is roughly the same as the actual median age of retirement among current retirees, which stands at 60.6 years of age.

Half of those who would prefer to retire before the normal retirement age for their employment would like to retire under the age of 55. Another 29% would like to retire between the ages of 55 and 59, and 20% would like to retire when they are 60 or older. The median age of preferred retirement among this group is 54 years. Among those who would prefer to either work part-time or take a less demanding job instead of retiring, 21% would like to change jobs before they turn 55, and another 15% would like to change jobs before they turn 60.

Observation:

The findings in Chapter I suggest that the pressures on government and business for increased retirement income benefits — stemming from an increase in the number of retirees and from inflation — are likely to mount considerably in the upcoming years. But the findings here suggest the cloud may have a silver lining. In the long run, more and more people are likely to defer retirement and work until a later age. This may greatly lessen the burden of retirement income costs on government and business: while the trend is strongly suggested by the findings, however, it should not be viewed as a sure-fire safeguard that will balance the pressures for increased retirement benefits. These pressures are likely to be strong, and business and government would be well-advised to seek active solutions to the problem.

Table II-5

PREFERRED AGE OF RETIREMENT, EARLY RETIREMENT, OR JOB CHANGE**
(Asked of those who prefer to retire or change jobs)

Q.: And at what age would you prefer to (retire/retire before normal retirement/take a less demanding job)?

(Number of respondents)	Retire At Normal Age (335)	Retire Before Normal Age (295)	Continue To Work Part-time Or At A Less Demanding Job (473)
	%	%	%
Under 55	15	50	21
55-59	17	29	15
60	15	8	11
61-62	19	8	7
63-64	2	1	2
65	27	3	16
66-70	2	—	8
71-75	—	—	2
Over 75	*	—	2
Haven't decided yet	1	1	6
It depends	1	1	6
Not sure	1	*	3
Median age	60.2	54.0	61.2

*Less than 0.5%.

**The columns in this table represent those who say, in response to the question on Table II-4, that they would prefer to retire at a normal age, retire before a normal age, or continue to work at some type of less demanding job instead of retiring. As seen here, there is a wide range of opinion about the preferred age of retirement among those who say they would prefer to retire at a normal retirement age.

Intended Retirement Alternatives

Table II-6 shows the retirement alternatives current employees think they are actually most likely to choose, and provides a comparison with the retirement preferences shown in Table II-4. Overall, there is little difference between what employees say they intend to do about retirement and what they would prefer to do.

Nearly 1 out of 3 workers (32%) plan to retire when they reach the normal retirement age for their job. This is slightly more than the percentage who would prefer to retire at the normal retirement age. Interestingly, only 15% plan to retire before the normal retirement age, 7 points less than the percentage who would prefer to do so.

There is virtually no change between the percentage of people who would prefer to continue working instead of retiring (51%) and the percentage who actually plan to continue working instead of retiring (49%).

As with preferred retirement alternatives, actual retirement plans vary significantly with the type of current employment. Although the data are not shown here, the self-employed are far more likely to plan to continue working instead of retiring than are wage workers or salaried workers. A high 73% of those who are currently self-employed plan to continue to work part-time or full-time, compared with 44% of hourly wage workers and 48% of salaried workers.

Lastly, pension coverage is an important factor in retirement plans. People covered by public pension plans, for instance, are less likely than those covered by private pensions to plan to continue working full-time as long as possible. However, they are more likely to plan to retire at a normal or early retirement age and take a job with another employer. This is not surprising if one considers the early retirement age permitted by many public plans. People who are not covered by any type of pension plan are more likely than others to defer retirement, with 56% planning to continue working in one capacity or another as long as possible. Among those covered by private pensions, 34% plan to retire when they reach normal retirement age, and 46% plan to continue working instead of retiring.

The age at which employees say they are most likely to retire is slightly higher than the age at which they would prefer to retire. Those who plan to retire at normal retirement age plan to do so at a median age of 62.5 years, and 40% of this group plan to retire at 65. Employees who plan to retire before the normal retirement age plan to do so at a median age of 56.6 years.

Observation:

The results in this section strongly suggest that deferred retirement age is likely to become a reality. The data do not suggest that the change will happen overnight — significant numbers of people look forward to retirement and many plan to retire as soon as or before they reach the normal retirement age. But it is clearly a possibility in the not-too-distant future. Many current workers show a preference for working during retirement. This preference for working is likely to be spurred by a number of other factors conducive to a longer working life. For instance, as the number of white collar jobs that do not require physical strength increase, more people will be capable of working into their later years. And as inflation continues to erode the purchasing power of retirees, many are likely to continue working out of economic necessity.

The findings have important implications for business. The growing number of older workers in the work force will call for some rethinking about the way the working process is structured. Older workers will be looking for tasks that are less demanding but that utilize their skills and experience. Also, part-time employment is likely to become considerably more widespread than it is today. The number of younger people entering the work force is likely to shrink during the 1980's. Employers are likely to welcome the increased interest in working among older workers, but they will have to be prepared to make changes to meet the special employment needs of an aging work force.

Table II-6

MOST LIKELY RETIREMENT ARRANGEMENT
(Asked of current employees)

Q.: Now which **one** of the things on this list are you actually most likely to do?

(Number of respondents)	Total (1316)	Covered By Private Pension Plan (692)	Covered By Public Pension Plan (228)	Not Covered By Pension Plan (448)
	%	%	%	%
Retire when I reach the normal retirement age for my employment	32	34	33	29
Instead of retiring, continue to work part-time as long as I can	23	21	20	27
Retire before I reach the normal retirement age for my employment	15	18	15	11
Instead of retiring, continue to work full-time as long as I can at the same job and the same pay	14	14	11	18
Retire at a normal or early retirement age for my employment and take a job with another employer	8	8	15	4
Instead of retiring, continue to work full-time as long as I can at a less demanding job with less pay	4	3	4	7
Other	1	1	2	1
Not sure	2	2	1	3

Table II-7

INTENDED AGE OF RETIREMENT OR JOB CHANGE
(Asked of those who intend to retire or change jobs)

Q.: And at what age are you most likely to (retire/take a less demanding job)?

(Number of respondents)	Retire At Normal Age (417)	Retire Before Normal Age (202)	Continue To Work Part-time Or At A Less Demanding Job (45)
	%	%	%
Under 55	6	36	17
55-59	10	32	12
60	9	5	13
61-62	21	16	8
63-64	3	1	2
65	40	8	23
66-70	4	—	8
71-75	*	—	2
Over 75	*	—	3
Haven't decided yet	1	2	5
It depends	2	—	4
Not sure	2	1	2
Median age	62.5	56.6	60.5

*Less than 0.5%.

Employment and Current Retirees

At the time this survey was taken, 81% of retirees interviewed were not employed. Eight percent were employed part-time, and 5% were employed full-time.

Table II-8

CURRENT EMPLOYMENT STATUS AMONG RETIREES
(Asked of retired employees)

Q.: What is your current employment status — are you employed full-time, employed part-time, not presently employed, or what?

(Number of respondents)	Total Retired Employees (379)
	%
Employed full-time	5
Employed part-time	8
Not presently employed	81
None of the above	
Student	*
Military services	—
Housewife	5
Other	*

*Less than 0.5%.

Nearly half (46%) of today's retirees would prefer to be working, while an even half (50%) would not.

Not surprisingly, retirees who do not receive pension benefits — those who are most severely affected by financial pressure — are more likely to want to work during retirement than are those who are receiving pension benefits. More interesting, perhaps, is the finding that preferences to work during retirement are equally widespread among lower, middle and upper income groups. Forty-nine percent of retirees earning less than $7,000 per year would prefer to be working, as would 45% earning between $7,000 and $14,999, and 48% earning $15,000 per year and over.

Also, though the sample is too small for reliable analysis, it seems that the findings suggest that many retirees who are working prefer to be working. Forty-two percent of those who are not working would like to be doing so.

Observation:

These findings suggest two important motivations for working during retirement. The first is the psychological benefits derived from working. Most employed retirees seem to be working because they want to, not because they have to. And preferences for work are high among all income groups, not just those where the need for additional income is the greatest. One of the major problems faced by retirees — particularly those who are financially secure — is the feeling of uselessness and idleness that comes when they are no longer working. For many, working during retirement is an important way to maintain one's self-esteem and self-worth.

But clearly economic need is also an incentive to keep working. Many of those in lower income brackets would prefer to work more for reasons of economics than for psychological fulfillment. This is particularly true among retirees who do not receive pension benefits. And there is reason to believe that preferences to work during retirement — whether motivated by psychological or economic needs — are not demonstrated fully by the survey. Ironically, among low- and middle-income retirees who might benefit most from working, the economic disincentives to work imposed by the Social Security laws may be masking desires that would otherwise surface. As the rules governing retirement employment and Social Security are liberalized, and as the financial pressures on retirees continue to mount, more and more retirees are likely to seek employment.

Table II-9

PREFERENCE FOR EMPLOYMENT AMONG RETIRED EMPLOYEES
(Asked of retired employees)

Q.: (Do you) (Would you) prefer to work now, or not?

(Number of respondents)	Total (396)	Receiving Pension Benefits (297)	Not Receiving Pension Benefits (96)	Employment Status		Income		
				Employed* (47)	Not Employed (358)	Under $7,000 (139)	$7,000-$14,999 (150)	$15,000 And Over (99)
	%	%	%	%	%	%	%	%
Do/would prefer to work	46	40	52	85	42	49	45	48
Do/would not prefer to work	50	58	42	15	54	50	53	40
Not sure	4	3	6	—	4	2	3	11

*Sample too small for reliable analysis.

Not only would significant numbers of retired people prefer to work, but more than half would have preferred to continue working instead of retiring. Asked to assume that they had an adequate retirement income, 31% of current retirees would have preferred to retire when they reached the normal retirement age. Interestingly, if one considers the current trend toward early retirement, only 12% would have preferred to retire before they reached the normal retirement age. The remaining 53% would have preferred to continue in some kind of employment:

- 4% would have preferred to retire at a normal or early retirement age and to have taken a job with another employer.

- 22% would have preferred to continue to work full-time at the same job for the same pay as long as possible, instead of retiring.

- 4% would have preferred to continue to work full-time at a less demanding job at less pay for as long as possible, instead of retiring.

- 23% would have preferred to continue to work part-time for as long as possible.

Finally, it is interesting to note that more than 1 out of 5 of today's retirees retired under the age of 55, and 34% retired at 60 or younger. The mean age of retirement among today's retirees is 61.5 years.

Table II-10

PREFERRED RETIREMENT ALTERNATIVES
(Asked of retired employees)

Q.: Here is a list of things that people do about work when they get on in years. In retrospect, assuming you would have had an adequate amount of retirement income, which **one** of the things on this list would you have preferred to do when you retired?

(Number of respondents)	Total (391)	Receiving Pension Benefits (292)	Not Receiving Pension Benefits (95)
	%	%	%
Retired when you reached the normal age for your employment	31	36	30
Retired before you reached the normal retirement age for your employment	12	15	10
Retired at normal or early retirement age for your employment and taken a job with another employer	4	8	2
Instead of retiring, continued to work full-time as long as you could at the same job and the same pay	22	15	24
Instead of retiring, continued to work full-time as long as you could at a less demanding job with less pay	4	7	3
Instead of retiring continued to work part-time as long as you could	23	17	27
Other	2	1	2
Not sure	2	1	2

Table II-11

AGE OF RETIREMENT
(Asked of retired employees)

Q.: And at what age did you actually retire?

(Number of respondents)	Total (393)
	%
Under 55	21
55-59	8
60	5
61-62	21
63-64	9
65	22
66-70	11
71-75	1
Over 75	2
It depends	—
Not sure	*
Median age	60.6

*Less than 0.5%.

CHAPTER III:

PLANNING FOR RETIREMENT

The Importance of Retirement Planning

Pre-retirement planning is perhaps the single most important factor in assuring a comfortable retirement life free from financial worries. As will be shown, many current retirees who are less than satisfied with the quality of their retired life, or who have inadequate retirement incomes, attribute their situation to inadequate pre-retirement planning.

Only 29% of current retirees feel they had done enough planning for their retirement. The remaining 70% feel that their pre-retirement planning was in some way inadequate: 26% feel they had done some but not enough planning for a comfortable retirement; 10% had done far too little planning; and a sizeable 34% had done no planning at all.

One of the key factors in adequate retirement planning, according to the experience of current retirees, is having some type of pension plan to provide income during old age. More than 4 out of 10 (42%) of those receiving pension benefits felt they had done enough planning before retirement, but just 2 in 10 (20%) of those not receiving pension benefits make the same claim.

Table III-1

AMOUNT OF PLANNING DONE FOR RETIREMENT
(Asked of retired employees)

Q.: How much planning did you do for retirement — enough planning to have a comfortable retirement, some planning but not enough, far too little planning, or no planning at all?

(Number of respondents)	Total (395)	Receiving Pension Benefits (295)	Not Receiving Pension Benefits (95)
	%	%	%
Enough	29	42	20
Some but not enough	26	25	27
Far too little	10	9	10
No planning at all	34	22	42
Not sure	*	1	—

*Less than 0.5%.

Retirement Planning and Current Employees

Unfortunately for many retirees, the importance of pre-retirement planning was not fully discovered until after retirement. The survey results show that the same dilemma will be faced by many of today's workers when they retire. Only 1 in 3 (33%) of today's workers feel they have done enough planning for retirement considering their present age, and a full two-thirds admit that they have done less than enough planning.

Somewhat ironically, those who have done the least pre-retirement planning are the people likely to need it the most. Hourly wage workers — those who are looking forward to an early retirement more than any other group — have done the least planning for retirement. Thirty-five percent of all wage workers admit they have done less than enough planning for retirement considering their present age, and a sizeable 41% claim they have done no planning at all. Only 24% of this group feel they have done enough pre-retirement planning considering their present age. At the other end of the spectrum are self-employed workers, a large majority of whom intend to work as long as possible. Forty-two percent (42%) of these workers feel they have done enough planning considering their present age, 42% feel they have done some but not enough, and only 17% say they have done no planning at all.

Predictably, younger workers have done less planning for retirement than older workers. But the surprising finding here is that many older workers have done less planning than they feel necessary for a comfortable retirement. Among workers between the ages of 50 and 64, 20% have done no planning at all, and 42% have done some but not enough considering their present age. Just 38% have done what they feel is enough planning for retirement considering their present age.

Table III-2

AMOUNT OF PLANNING FOR RETIREMENT
(Asked of current employees)

Q.: First I'd like to ask you some questions about retirement. How much planning would you say you've done for your retirement — enough planning considering your present age, some but not enough planning considering your present age, or no planning at all?

		Employment			Age			
(Number of respondents)	Total (1330)	Hourly Wage Worker (541)	Salaried (599)	Self-Employed (160)	18-24 (150)	25-34 (379)	35-49 (431)	50-64 (339)
	%	%	%	%	%	%	%	%
Enough considering present age	33	24	39	42	21	30	34	38
Some but not enough considering present age	37	35	38	42	24	36	40	42
No planning at all	30	41	23	17	54	34	26	20
Not sure	*	1	*	—	1	1	*	*

*Less than 0.5%.

The importance of pre-retirement planning in providing an adequate income for later years is demonstrated clearly by the findings in Table III-3.

In total, 41% of the retirees interviewed feel they have a standard of living that is less than adequate. However, among those who feel they had done enough retirement planning, only 10% claim to have a less than adequate standard of living. The difference between this group and retirees who feel they have done less than enough planning is remarkable. Fifty-two percent (52%) of those who have done some but not enough planning, and 56% of those who have done far too little or no planning before retirement, have incomes that are less than adequate today.

Table III-3

RETIREMENT PLANNING AND INCOME ADEQUACY
(Asked of retired employees)

Q.: Overall, does your present income provide you with a more than adequate standard of living, an adequate standard of living, or a less than adequate standard of living?

(Number of respondents)	Total (405)	Pre-Retirement Planning		
		Enough (116)	Some But Not Enough (104)	Far Too Little Or None (180)
	%	%	%	%
More than adequate	13	23	5	11
Adequate	46	67	43	33
Less than adequate	41	10	52	56
Not sure	*	—	1	—

*Less than 0.5%.

Current and Expected Sources of Retirement Income

Table III-4 shows the major sources of income among today's retirees, and the consequences — in terms of where retirement income will come from — of inadequate pre-retirement planning.

The primary source of income for today's retirees is Social Security, with 83% claiming to receive Social Security benefits. Retirees also rely heavily on various types of pension plan benefits, though, as a whole, pension benefits rank a distant second to Social Security in terms of the number of people who rely on them for income. Company plans claim the highest number of benefits recipients (20%), followed by government plans (16%), union plans (5%), individual retirement accounts (2%), employee thrift or savings plans (2%), and profit sharing (1%). Relied on by 1 in 3 retirees (33%), personal savings accounts are the third most important source of retirement income. Additionally, 8% of today's retirees rely on money from their children or other relatives, and 7% depend on supplemental security income.

Observation:

The results here further demonstrate the importance of pre-retirement planning in ensuring an adequate income. While sizeable majorities of retirees collect Social Security benefits regardless of how well they planned for retirement, those who fail to do enough planning for retirement can count on fewer sources of retirement income; people who have planned well for their retirement are more than twice as likely than those who have not, to be able to depend on personal savings, various types of pension benefits, and other personal income sources such as investments in stocks or bonds and real estate investments. And the less planning people do, the more likely they are to have to rely on sources such as supplemental security income and their children or other relatives.

Table III-4

CURRENT SOURCES OF RETIREMENT INCOME
(Asked of retired employees)

Q.: Here is a list of sources of retirement income. From which of these sources are you currently receiving income?

(Number of respondents)	Total (395)	Amount Of Retirement Planning		
		More Than Adequate (150)	Adequate (138)	Less Than Adequate (107)
	%	%	%	%
Social Security	83	82	87	78
Personal savings account at a bank	33	45	36	17
Company pension plan benefits	20	29	18	12
Government pension plan benefits	16	25	16	9
Investments in stocks or bonds	11	22	5	9
Real estate investment	11	22	9	2
Money from children or other relatives	8	2	14	5
Supplemental security income	7	4	7	10
Union pension plan benefits	5	5	5	4
Earnings from new employment after retiring from current job	5	7	4	4
Savings from an employee thrift or savings plan	2	4	2	1
Individual retirement account benefits	2	6	2	—
Profit sharing plan benefits	1	2	1	1
Proceeds from insurance	1	2	1	—
Inheritance	*	2	—	1
Keogh Plan benefits	—	—	—	—
Other	1	1	1	1
None	3	1	1	6
Not sure	—	—	—	—

*Less than 0.5%.

Members of today's work force are considerably more likely to be counting on receiving pension benefits during their retirement than were today's retirees. Six of every ten full-time workers claim to be covered by a private pension plan, and more than 2 in 10 (23%) are covered by a government pension plan. In addition to widespread participation in pension plans, of course, an overwhelming majority of the work force (93%) are covered by Social Security.

Expectedly, pension plan participation is most widespread among older workers, and least widespread among those in the younger age groups. More than 1 in every 4 (28%) workers between the ages of 50 and 64 are covered by a government pension plan, and more than 6 in 10 (62%) are covered by a private plan. The same plans cover just 9% and 43%, respectively, of workers in the 18-to-24 age group.

Table III-5

RETIREMENT INCOME PLAN COVERAGE AMONG CURRENT EMPLOYEES
(Asked of current employees)

Q.: Are you covered by (ITEM)?

(Number of respondents)	Total (1281)	Age 18-24 (145)	25-34 (363)	35-49 (416)	50-64 (332)
	%	%	%	%	%
Social Security	93	91	88	95	95
A private pension plan	60	43	57	69	62
A government pension plan	23	9	21	25	28

The following two tables show the expected sources of retirement income among those currently employed full-time. Importantly, the results suggest that sizeable proportions of today's work force have done relatively little pre-retirement planning, and that many — even older workers close to retirement age — are ill-prepared for retirement from a financial standpoint.

Since the coming of Social Security in the 1930's, the provision of retirement income in the United States has been based on the principle of the three-legged stool. The idea is that the government, through Social Security, will provide a basic level of retirement income that will supplement other income sources, such as a pension and personal savings. While most people expect to receive Social Security (87%), a substantial minority do not expect to receive income from a pension plan, and a majority do not expect to rely on personal savings. Only 40% (Table III-6) expect to rely on savings. In total (Table III-7), 75% expect to receive retirement income from some type of pension plan, including public and private pensions, profit sharing plans, IRAs, Keogh Plans, and employee thrift plans. However, 25% do not expect income from any of these sources. Most of this latter group (23%) expect to rely on Social Security as their primary source of retirement income.

Among those who expect to receive some type of pension benefit, most expect to receive company pension benefits (43%), followed by government plan benefits (14%), union plan, profit sharing, and employee thrift plan benefits (10% each), Individual Retirement Account benefits (9%), and Keogh Plan benefits (3%).

Many workers expect to rely heavily on other personal income sources: investment in stocks or bonds (20%); real estate investment (19%); proceeds from insurance (17%); and earnings from post-retirement employment (11%). Expectations for income from post-retirement employment are highest among those covered by public plans (15%), which frequently permit employees to retire after 20 years of service. Also, not shown in the table, expectations for income from post-retirement employment are highest among younger workers (17% in the 18-to-24 year age group), and lowest among those closest to retirement (8% among those in the 50-to-64 year age group). This is further evidence of a possible long-term trend toward later retirement.

Relatively small percentages of those who are not currently covered by a pension plan expect to become covered sometime before they retire. However, most do not expect to participate in a pension plan. Also, employees in this group are no more likely to expect income from other sources such as personal savings accounts, earnings from post-retirement employment, insurance, or investments than are workers who expect to receive pension plan benefits.

Table III-6

EXPECTED SOURCES OF INCOME AFTER RETIREMENT
(Asked of current employees)

Q.: Here is a list of sources of retirement income. From which of these sources do you expect to receive income when you finally retire?

| | | Plan Coverage | | |
| | Total (1322) | Covered By Private Plan (693) | Covered By Public Plan (231) | Not Covered (450) |
(Number of respondents)	%	%	%	%
Social Security benefits	87	89	74	90
Company pension plan benefits	43	67	28	17
Personal savings account at a bank	40	41	32	41
Investments in stocks or bonds	20	23	18	15
Real estate investment	19	18	18	20
Proceeds from insurance	17	20	19	13
Government pension plan benefits	14	6	75	3
Earnings from new employment after retiring from current job	11	10	15	11
Savings from an employee thrift or savings plan	10	13	11	6
Profit sharing plan benefits	10	14	2	6
Union pension plan benefits	10	14	7	6
Individual retirement account benefits	9	12	7	5
Inheritance	7	5	6	9
Keogh Plan benefits	3	4	1	2
Money from children or other relatives	1	*	1	2
Other	4	4	7	3
None	*	*	—	1
Not sure	*	*	*	*

*Less than 0.5%.

As previously mentioned, 75% of those currently employed expect to receive pension benefits when they retire. Except for those between 18 and 24 years of age, who have given much less thought to retirement than other groups, expectations for pension benefits are consistent throughout all age groups. Virtually every employee who expects to receive pension benefits expects Social Security benefits as well.

Nearly 1 out of every 4 workers who are currently employed full-time expect to rely on Social Security and not a pension as their primary source of retirement income. While this situation occurs most frequently in the youngest age grouping, it should be noted that a sizeable 22% of those between 50 and 64 years of age expect to rely primarily on Social Security in retirement. Lastly, 34% of those not covered by a pension plan expect to be covered by the time they retire. However, more than 6 in 10 (61%) expect to rely on Social Security without a pension.

Table III-7

MULTIPLE SOURCES OF RETIREMENT INCOME
(Asked of current employees)

Q.: Here is a list of sources of retirement income. From which of these sources do you expect to receive income when you finally retire?

		Age				Not Covered By
(Number of respondents)	Total (1290)	18-24 (148)	25-34 (364)	35-49 (421)	50-64 (334)	Pension Plan (428)
	%	%	%	%	%	%
Pension*	75	65	76	77	77	34
Pension and Social Security	64	54	61	69	69	29
Social Security and no pension	23	33	20	21	22	61

*Includes private and public plans, profit sharing, employee thrift plans, Individual Retirement Accounts and Keogh Plans.

The Amount and Adequacy of Expected Retirement Income

Not only have the bulk of those currently employed done an inadequate amount of planning for retirement, but a sizeable majority have not given any thought to the basic question of how much money they will need during retirement. While 1 in 3 among the working public claim to have given some thought to this matter, a surprisingly high 58% have not. Even more surprising, perhaps, is the finding that nearly half of those who are between 50 and 64 years of age have not given any thought to how much money they will need when they finally retire.

Table III-8

WHETHER GIVEN THOUGHT TO AMOUNT OF MONEY REQUIRED AFTER RETIREMENT
(Asked of current employees)

Q.: Have you given any thought to how much money you will need when you finally retire, or not?

		Age			
(Number of respondents)	Total (1297)	18-24 (148)	25-34 (367)	35-49 (423)	50-64 (335)
	%	%	%	%	%
Have given thought	36	22	31	37	45
Have not given thought	58	73	64	56	48
Not sure	6	5	4	7	6

When asked how much they think they will need when they retire, the working public report a need for a median of $851 a month. Reflecting their interest in retaining their pre-retirement standard of living, employees in higher income groups feel they will need more income during retirement than employees in lower income groups. Also, it should be noted that more than 1 of every 4 workers (27%) are not sure how much they will need during retirement, and, though it is not reported here, the percentage of employees who are not sure of their retirement income needs is a strikingly high 31% among those in the 50-to-64 year age bracket.

Table III-9

REQUIRED MONTHLY INCOME DURING RETIREMENT
(Asked of current employees)

Q.: Ignoring future inflation, how much income do you think you personally are going to need per month when you finally retire?

			Income		
(Number of respondents)	Total (1243)	Under $7,000 (87)	$7,000-$14,999 (375)	$15,000-$24,999 (470)	$25,000 And Over (261)
	%	%	%	%	%
$1-$300	3	10	4	2	1
$301-$600	19	30	28	16	10
$601-$900	17	13	19	20	13
$901-$1,200	21	9	15	27	27
$1,201-$1,500	6	3	3	8	7
$1,501-$2,000	4	—	2	3	9
$2,001-$3,000	2	1	1	1	5
$3,001-$4,000	*	—	—	*	2
$4,001-$5,000	*	—	1	—	2
$5,001 and over	*	—	—	*	—
Not sure	27	34	27	24	24
Median	$851	$534	$667	$905	$1,055

*Less than 0.5%.

At present, 7 out of 10 of the working public able to estimate their retirement income feel that it will be adequate, though 23% feel their income will be less than adequate. By 79-17%, those covered by a private pension plan are particularly confident about having an adequate income during retirement. Interestingly, 59% of those without a pension believe their retirement income will be adequate while 33% believe it will not.

Earlier it was shown that 41% of today's retirees believe their income is less than adequate. Although not shown on the table, this dropped to 23% among retirees receiving pension benefits, but rose to a high 56% among those not receiving pension benefits. On the basis of these findings, it would seem that many in today's work force who are not covered by a pension plan are seriously misjudging the amount and adequacy of their retirement income.

Table III-10

ADEQUACY OF EXPECTED RETIREMENT INCOME TO
PROVIDE DESIRED STANDARD OF LIVING
(Asked of those able to estimate their retirement income)

Q.: And as far as you know, will the amount of income you are likely to get during retirement provide a very adequate, somewhat adequate, somewhat inadequate, or very inadequate income in terms of providing the standard of living that you would like?

(Number of respondents)	Total (1059)	Covered By Private Pension Plan (563)	Covered By Public Pension Plan (195)	Not Covered By Pension Plan (346)
	%	%	%	%
Very adequate	18	24	16	12
Somewhat adequate	52	55	55	47
Somewhat inadequate	16	13	19	19
Very inadequate	7	4	6	14
Not sure	6	4	4	9

Observation:

These findings are an early warning of potential trouble ahead for government and employers, but most of all, for future retirees. Pre-retirement planning will not provide a 100% guarantee of a secure retirement, but the experience of current retirees makes it clear that early retirement planning is a critically important ingredient for a happy retirement free from financial hardship. Yet many of today's employees are not aware of its importance. Many expect Social Security to be a primary source of retirement income, and well less than half of today's work force expect to rely on savings during retirement. Additionally, surprisingly large percentages of the working public of all ages have not given any serious thought to how much money they will need when they retire.

The findings strongly imply that government, employers, and pension experts should focus considerable attention on making current employees aware of their potential retirement needs and the importance of early pre-retirement planning. Hopefully the findings reported here on the experiences and difficulties faced by today's retirees will help spur others to seriously consider and begin planning for their retirement.

What is needed is a kind of preventive medicine for retirees, where clearly "an ounce of prevention is worth a pound of cure." Social Security, employers, public and private pension plans, taxpayers, and the economy as a whole — each of these will be subject to increasing pressure as the number of retirees — many of whom will be pushing to retain their pre-retirement standard of living — continues to expand into the next century. By focusing public attention on the problem now, many of the potentially serious and undoubtedly costly consequences of inadequate pre-retirement planning can be avoided.

Retirement Income Responsibility: The Three-Legged Stool

Since the 1930's, this country's policies toward the welfare of its retirees has been based on the concept of the three-legged stool — the idea that the economic security of retirees should be shared jointly by the government, private industry, and employees themselves. Although this principle may underlie many current retirement income policies, it is not an idea that is widely understood by either employees or the business community.

Fifty-four percent of current and retired employees believe retirees themselves should be at least partly responsible for their economic security during retirement: 24% feel responsibility rests solely with retirees: 7% feel it rests with government and retirees: 11% feel it rests with the retirees' employer or union along with retirees themselves: 12% believe the responsibility should be shared by government, the retirees' employer or union, and the retirees themselves. In total, 46% believe the government should be at least partly responsible for the economic security of retirees, and 42% feel that business should be at least partly responsible.

It should be noted here that 46% of the respondents do not mention that retirees should be responsible for providing for their own economic security, and only 12% believe the responsibility should be shared by government, employers or unions, and retirees.

The three-legged stool has a larger but still small percentage of adherents among business executives. Just 30% believe that responsibility for the economic security of retirees should be shared by government, employers, and retirees themselves.

To a considerable extent, employers accept their share of the responsibility for the economic security of their retirees. Seventy-two percent believe employers should be at least partly responsible for providing retirement income for employees. Another 23%, however, believe the retirees themselves should be responsible. The greatest consensus among business leaders exists for exclusion of government from retirement income responsibility. Only 1% feel the government should be solely responsible for retirees' economic security and only 5% feel that companies and government should share the responsibility.

Table III-11

WHO SHOULD PROVIDE RETIREES' ECONOMIC SECURITY
(Asked of current and retired employees and of business leaders)

Q.: In general, who should be responsible for providing for the economic security of retirees — the government, the retirees' former employers or union, or the retirees themselves and their families, or a combination of these?

(Number of respondents)	Total (1690)	Current And Retired Employees Age					Total Business Leaders (205)
		18-24 (150)	25-34 (378)	35-49 (437)	50-64 (422)	65 And Over (302)	
	%	%	%	%	%	%	%
Government only	20	23	15	15	21	24	1
Retirees' employer or union only	12	15	10	13	10	11	3
Retirees themselves	24	19	23	26	23	28	23
Government and retirees' employer or union	7	8	9	8	7	6	5
Government and retirees themselves	7	5	8	8	7	6	2
Retirees' employer or union and retirees themselves	11	13	14	12	10	7	34
Government and retirees' employer and retirees themselves	12	8	15	14	13	8	30
Not sure	7	7	5	5	6	10	1

31

Moreover, a majority of current and retired employees and business leaders are not satisfied with the balance of retirement income that is currently provided by Social Security, pensions, and personal savings. Slightly more than 1 in 4 (27%) of current and retired employees feel that the balance of income provided by these sources is about right as it is. But a 57% majority feel that one or two should provide more income than they do now. Business leaders are somewhat more satisfied with the status quo than are employees and retirees, but an even 50% feel that one or two sources should provide more retirement income than they do now.

Those in the two groups who feel the balance to be wrong have diametrically opposed views as to which sources should provide more than they are providing now. A plurality (43%) of current and retired employees in the sample feel that Social Security should provide more income than it is currently providing. Another 16% feel pensions should provide more retirement income, and only 9% feel additional money should come from a retiree's personal savings.

Most business leaders who feel the current balance of retirement income is out of line look to personal savings (35%) to provide additional income. Only 8% feel Social Security should provide additional retirement income, and 15% look to pensions for additional funds.

Table III-12

ADEQUACY OF CURRENT SOURCES OF RETIREMENT INCOME
(Asked of current and retired employees and of business leaders)

Q.: Right now, income for people who are retired comes primarily from Social Security, pensions, and personal savings. Would you say that the balance of income from these three sources is about right as it is, or should one or two of the sources provide more income than they do now?

Q.: And which one or ones should provide more than they do now?

(Number of respondents)	Total Current And Retired Employees (1691)	Total Business Leaders (212)
	%	%
Balance is right	27	39
One or two should provide more	57	50
Not sure	17	10
Sources which should provide more		
Social Security	43	8
Pensions	16	15
Personal savings	9	35
Other	*	—
Not sure	2	3

*Less than 0.5%.

Observation:

These are critical findings, as they demonstrate that the principle which underlies much of the nation's retirement income policies is not fully understood by the public. Ideally, employees and retirees see the gov-

ernment, via Social Security, providing a greater share of retirement income than it does now. One in five believes the government alone should be responsible for the economic security of retirees. At the same time, while many believe that retirees themselves should be all or in part responsible for their own retirement income, few people believe more retirement income should be sought from personal savings. The principle of the three-legged stool has a somewhat higher percentage of adherents among business leaders, though of those who would alter the balance, many would decrease government's involvement in retirement income and place more responsibility on retirees themselves.

These findings are critical because they underlie many of the problems faced by today's retirees, and they presage even greater difficulties for the retirees of tomorrow. A surprising number of people do not understand the fundamental principle of the three-legged stool, and look either to government, their employer, or both to take care of them during retirement.

Knowledge of Private Pension Plans

An integral part of planning for retirement is an understanding of what is required and what is provided by various sources of retirement income. Yet sizeable percentages of the working public, whether participating in a private or public plan, or expecting Social Security benefits, do not know what their monthly benefit will be from these retirement income sources.

The working public is least likely to know what its benefits from Social Security will be. A total of 84% do not know what the size of their monthly Social Security benefit will be upon retirement. Again, the percentage who do not know the approximate size of their benefit is higher among younger workers, but it is of some concern to note that a sizeable 78% of the 50 to 64 year olds are unsure what their Social Security benefits will be.

Forty-six percent (46%) of those in government plans and 37% of those in private plans know what their benefit will be when they retire. Still, in almost every age grouping, more than half of today's employees do not know the size of their monthly retirement benefit.

Table III-13

KNOWLEDGE OF MONTHLY BENEFIT FROM RETIREMENT INCOME SERVICE
(Asked of those current employees covered by each retirement income source)

Q.: Do you know about what your monthly benefit from (ITEM) will be when you retire, or not?

(Number of respondents)	Government Plan					Private Plan					Social Security				
		Age					Age					Age			
	Total (216)	18-24 (9)*	25-34 (61)	35-49 (72)	50-64 (70)	Total (664)	18-24 (57)	25-34 (180)	35-49 (244)	50-64 (175)	Total (1170)	18-24 (131)	25-34 (318)	35-49 (387)	50-64 (311)
	%	%	%	%	%	%	%	%	%	%	%	%	%	%	%
Know benefit	46	30	41	56	40	37	21	38	34	41	17	5	13	17	22
Do not know	40	20	51	27	49	48	59	47	53	40	69	78	74	70	60
Not sure	14	40	8	15	12	15	18	14	13	18	15	17	13	13	18

*Sample too small for reliable analysis.

Employees should also be aware of their pension plans' vesting requirements. The topic of vesting is too complicated to be fully explored in a public survey; however, the findings here suggest that those involved in private plans have a fairly good if sometimes unclear understanding of their plans' vesting requirements.

Fifty-five percent (55%) of the working public covered by a private pension plan believe they would be able to receive or transfer the benefits they have accrued if they left their company today, while 30% believe they would not be able to receive or transfer their benefits. While 15% are not sure about this question of vesting, a full 85% were able to answer the question.

Table III-14

ABILITY TO RECEIVE OR TRANSFER PENSION BENEFITS
UPON LEAVING COMPANY
(Asked of those current employees covered by a private pension plan)

Q.: As far as you know, if you left your company today, would you be able to **receive** or **transfer** the pension benefits you have accrued, either immediately or at some later date, or not?

(Number of respondents)	Total (594)
	%
Would be able	55
Would not be able	30
Not sure	15

Most business leaders (91%) believe their employees would know whether or not they are vested. Judging from the previous responses, business leaders have a fairly accurate view on this question.

Fifty-one percent (51%) of employees with private pension plans correctly understand that the number of years in service is the factor that determines whether or not they are eligible to receive pension benefits if they leave their company or union before retirement. Also, 18% believe age is a determining factor. This may be correct in many instances, since age can be a factor in determining pension eligibility. The remaining 31% are either incorrect or uncertain.

Table III-15

EMPLOYERS' ESTIMATES OF EMPLOYEES' KNOWLEDGE
OF WHETHER THEY ARE VESTED
(Asked of business leaders)

Q.: Would you say that most of your employees know if they are vested, or not?

(Number of respondents)	Total (211)
	%
Most know	91
Most do not know	9
Not sure	—

Table III-16

KNOWLEDGE OF PENSION BENEFITS ELIGIBILITY REQUIREMENTS
(Asked of those current employees covered by a private pension plan)

Q.: Do you know what determines whether or not you are eligible to receive pension benefits if you leave your company or union before retirement — is it your job level, your salary level, your age, your number of years in full service, or aren't you sure?

(Number of respondents)	Total (583)
	%
Job level	5
Salary	7
Age	18
Years in service	51
Other	2
Not sure	17

Fifty-six percent (56%) of those covered by private plans whose eligibility to collect benefits before retirement is determined by years of service believe that less than ten years of service is required. Nine percent (9%) believe between ten and fifteen years are necessary, 21% believe more than fifteen years are necessary, and 14% are unsure. The most common vesting schedule under ERISA provides for full vesting after ten years of service, with no vesting before that date. Thus a sizeable portion of those with private plans are wrong in their understanding of the number of years of service required for benefit eligibility. Under ERISA, an employee is generally fully vested after ten years of service. At the maximum, under the ERISA mandated 5 to 15 rule, an employee would be fully vested after fifteen years.

Table III-17

NUMBER OF YEARS REQUIRED FOR ELIGIBILITY TO COLLECT BENEFITS
(Asked of those current employees whose pre-retirement pension
eligibility is determined by years of service)

Q.: How many years of service are required for you to become eligible to collect benefits if you leave work before retirement?

(Number of respondents)	Total (324)	Covered By Private Plan (324)
	%	%
Less than 10	56	56
10-15	9	9
16-20	11	12
21-30	9	9
31 and over	1	1
Not sure	14	14
Mean number of years	10.0	10.0

Observation:

Many private pension plan participants are familiar with some of the basic provisions of their plan, but the results show that there is ample room for improvement in their knowledge. Most seem to know whether or not they are vested though substantial minorities are uncertain or incorrect about vesting criteria. Also, more than half are uncertain about the size of their monthly retirement benefit. Even among those who are relatively close to retirement (50 to 64 years old), 58% do not know the approximate size of their monthly retirement benefit.

To a considerable extent, the public's limited knowledge about their pension plans is their own doing. Under ERISA, plan participants automatically receive a summary plan description and annual report summary. They may also request a personal benefits statement which will contain information about the total benefits they have personally accrued and the portion, if any, that is vested. The problem, as will be seen in a following chapter, is that a sizeable minority of employees are not interested enough in their retirement, which is years away for many, or in their pension plan to take the time to read these disclosure statements. At the same time, however, this does not absolve either government, employers, or pension experts from seeing that pension plan participants are well-informed. Perhaps if participants are made to understand the importance of retirement planning and pensions, they themselves, along with the government, employers, and taxpayers, will be better off in the future.

Some Guidelines for Retirement Planning

Many of the problems faced by tomorrow's retirees can be avoided by listening to the advice of current retirees. Some of the more important pieces of advice they have to offer younger people are shown in Table III-18.

More than anything, employees should start planning early for retirement. This piece of advice is mentioned by nearly 1 of every 2 (49%) retirees interviewed. Almost equally important, current employees should not expect to rely solely on Social Security and a pension for their retirement income period. Forty-eight percent (48%) of today's retirees advise younger people to "make sure they have put away some savings so that they don't have to rely solely on Social Security and pensions." More than 2 out of 5 (44%) advise people to work for an employer with a good pension plan.

With fast-rising inflation, having a pension plan that provides benefits which increase with the cost of living is becoming increasingly important to retiring employees. Almost 1 of every 3 retirees (32%) advise current employees to see that their pension plans have such a cost-of-living provision. Also, 28% stress the importance of being covered by a pension plan, 27% warn employees to be prepared for the financial difficulties inherent in a work-stopping disability before normal retirement, and 24% offer the obvious but apparently often ignored advice to be sure that one's total retirement income is enough to live on.

On average, current retirees feel that planning for retirement should begin in one's mid-thirties.

Table III-18

MOST IMPORTANT ADVICE TO OFFER YOUNGER PEOPLE
(Asked of retired employees)

Q.: Which two or three of these pieces of advice would be most important to give to younger people?

(Number of respondents)	Total (384) %
Start planning early for retirement	49
Make sure they have put away some savings, so that they don't have to rely solely on Social Security and pensions	48
Work for an employer with a good pension plan	44
Make sure their pension plan provides benefits that increase with the cost of living	32
Make sure you're covered by a good pension plan and not rely only on Social Security and savings	28
Make sure your retirement income is sufficient to live on if you could no longer work because of disability	27
Make sure that total amount received in retirement is enough to live on	24
None	1
Not sure	2

Table III-19

AGE AT WHICH PLANNING FOR RETIREMENT SHOULD BEGIN
(Asked of retired employees)

Q.: At what age do you think people should begin planning for retirement?

(Number of respondents)	Total (396) %
Before 21	11
21-25	14
26-30	10
31-35	5
36-40	10
41-45	5
46-50	6
51-55	6
56-60	6
Older than 60	7
It depends	12
Not sure	6
Mean age	36.0

CHAPTER IV:

AN ASSESSMENT OF CURRENT SOURCES OF RETIREMENT INCOME

General Ratings of Major Sources of Retirement Income

Current and retired employees and business leaders were asked to provide an overall rating of four major sources of retirement income — private or company pension plans, government pension plans, union pension plans, and Social Security.

First ranked among these sources, in the view of current and retired employees, are government pension plans, which receive a 57-18% positive rating, and a relatively high 25% not sure. Next come private or company pension plans with a moderately positive rating of 43-35%, and 22% not sure. A plurality of the public (40%) are not sure how to rate union pension plans. However, the plans receive a 34-26% positive rating from those able to offer an opinion. Lastly, the public is strongly critical in its views of Social Security, with negative opinions coming from almost 2 of every 3 people interviewed.

Unlike the current and retired employees, who rate government pension plans over private pensions, business leaders give the highest general rating to private pension plans. A sizeable 84% of business leaders voice a positive view about private or company pension plans, compared with just 63% holding the same view toward government plans. Also, business leaders are more critical in their views toward union pensions than current and retired employees. Forty-eight percent give union pensions a negative rating, compared to 40% positive. Surprisingly, business leaders are slightly more positive than the employee and retiree group in their views toward Social Security, though they give the program an overwhelming 61-39% negative rating.

Table IV-1

RATINGS OF RETIREMENT INCOME SOURCES
(Asked of current and retired employees and of business leaders)

Q.: Overall, how would you rate (LIST) in the country — would you say they are excellent, pretty good, only fair or poor?

(Number of respondents)		Current and Retired Employees (1690)			Business Leaders (211)		
		Positive	Negative	Not Sure	Positive	Negative	Not Sure
Private or company pension plans	%	43	35	22	84	13	3
Government pension plans	%	57	18	25	63	26	10
Union pension plans	%	34	26	40	40	48	12
Social Security	%	30	65	5	39	61	1

Assessment of Major Sources of Retirement Income

By and large, the working public and retirees interviewed tend to be far more positive toward government pension plans and private plans than toward union plans or Social Security. Government plans are 1st ranked (43%) for providing the highest benefits, followed by private plans (20%), union plans (13%), and Social Security (10%). Private plans and government plans are thought to be the best run, followed at some distance by union plans and Social Security. While approximately 1 in 10 feel that private plans or union plans are most in need of change, Social Security is the primary focus of workers' and retirees' concern on this measure. A sizeable 53% feel that Social Security is the retirement source most in need of change.

If they had to choose one source for all their retirement income, 36% of workers and retirees would choose government pensions and 27% would choose private pensions. Only 15% would choose to have all their retirement income provided by Social Security, and a smaller 9% would opt for union pensions. Similarly, Social Security and union plans are the sources people would least prefer to rely on for all their retirement income.

Not only do a sizeable percentage of current and retired employees believe that government plans provide the highest benefits, but a plurality (33%) believe that they provide the highest benefits for the money contributed. Roughly 1 in 4 (24%) hold the same view about private plans. These views are at odds with those of business leaders, a large majority of whom (63%) feel that private or company plans provide the highest benefits for the money contributed.

Table IV-2

ASSESSMENTS OF SOURCES OF RETIREMENT INCOME
(Asked of current and retired employees)

Q.: Here is a list of the plans we've been discussing. Which one source on this list would you say generally provides the highest benefits to its beneficiaries?

Q.: In general, which one of these sources would you say is the best run?

Q.: And in general, which one is most in need of change for the better?

Q.: If you had to rely on just **one** of these sources for all your retirement income, which one would you most prefer?

Q.: Finally, which **one** of these sources would you **least** prefer to rely on for all your retirement income?

(Number of respondents)	Highest Benefits (1685) %	Best Run (1682) %	Need Of Change (1636) %	Most Prefer (1673) %	Least Prefer (1665) %
Private pension plans covering employees in private industry	20	30	9	27	11
Government pension plans covering federal, state and local government employees	43	29	6	36	4
Union pension plans	13	9	10	9	24
Social Security	10	10	53	15	37
None	*	1	1	1	1
Not sure	14	20	21	12	23

*Less than 0.5%.

39

Table IV-3

PLAN PROVIDING BEST BENEFITS FOR MONEY CONTRIBUTED
(Asked of current and retired employees and of business leaders)

Q.: Which one of these plans — private or company pensions, government pensions, union pensions or social security — provides the best benefits for the money contributed?

(Number of respondents)	Total Current And Retired Employees (1605) %	Total Business Leaders (210) %
Government pension plans	33	22
Private or company pension plans	24	63
Social Security	15	7
Union pension plans	11	3
Not sure	16	4

Like current and retired employees, business leaders are strongly negative in their views toward union plans and Social Security. But unlike employees, they are far more positive about private plans than government plans.

Business leaders differentiate between a plan which provides the highest benefits for the money contributed, and a plan which simply provides the highest benefits. Though they feel that private plans provide the highest benefits for the money contributed, a 62% majority feel that government plans provide the highest benefits. Only 22% feel that private pension plans provide the highest benefits of the plans listed. Current and retired employees do not make this distinction; substantial pluralities believe that government plans provide both the highest benefits and the highest benefits for the money contributed.

Business leaders have mixed views as to which source of retirement income is most in need of change. Exactly half feel that Social Security is most in need of change, while another 25% hold the same view about union plans, and 20% about government plans.

Interestingly, while more than half (58%) of the business leaders would recommend that employees rely on private plans if they had to rely on one plan for all their retirement income, more than 1 in 5 (21%) would recommend government pension plans, and nearly 1 in 5 (17%) would recommend Social Security. Union plans (49%) and Social Security (38%) are by far the plans least recommended for employees to rely on for all their retirement income.

Table IV-4

BUSINESS LEADER EVALUATIONS OF RETIREMENT INCOME SOURCES
(Asked of business leaders)

Q.: Now, which one source on this list would you say generally provides the highest benefits to its beneficiaries?

Q.: In general, which one of these sources would you say is the best run?

Q.: And in general, which one is most in need of change for the better?

Q.: If employees had to rely on just **one** of these sources for all their retirement income, which one would you personally recommend to them?

Q.: Finally, which **one** of these sources would you personally recommend to your employees to rely on for **all** their retirement income?

(Number of respondents: 212)	Highest Benefits	Best Run	Need of Change	Most Recommend	Least Recommend
	%	%	%	%	%
Private pension plans covering employees in private industry	22	87	1	58	3
Government pension plans covering federal, state and local government employees	62	6	20	21	4
Union pension plans	3	2	25	2	49
Social Security	7	3	50	17	38
None	—	—	—	—	1
Not sure	6	2	4	2	4

To a considerable extent, people's attitudes toward various retirement income sources are colored by their personal pension plan involvement. For instance, those participating in private plans feel private pension plans are best run and are the source they would most like to rely on for all their retirement income. Public employees feel the same way about government pension plans. The strongest degree of unanimity, however, is found in public attitudes toward the retirement income source most in need of change. Whether covered by a private plan, a public plan, or not covered by any pension plan at all, majorities of retired and current employees feel that Social Security is the program most in need of change.

Table IV-5

BEST-RUN SOURCE OF RETIREMENT INCOME
(Asked of current and retired employees)

Q.: In general, which one of these sources would you say is the best run?

(Number of respondents)	Total Current And Retired Employees (1682)	Current Employees			
		Total (1321)	Covered By Private Plan (693)	Covered By Public Plan (229)	Not Covered (453)
	%	%	%	%	%
Private pension plans covering employees in private industry	30	34	40	29	29
Government pension plans covering federal, state and local government employees	29	30	29	44	25
Union pension plans	9	10	9	9	13
Social Security	10	7	7	3	8
None	1	1	1	—	2
Not sure	20	18	14	15	22

Table IV-6

MOST PREFERRED SOURCE OF RETIREMENT INCOME
(Asked of current and retired employees)

Q.: If you had to rely on just **one** of these sources for all your retirement income, which one would you most prefer?

(Number of respondents)	Total Current And Retired Employees (1673)	Current Employees			
		Total (1314)	Covered By Private Plan (688)	Covered By Public Plan (228)	Not Covered (451)
	%	%	%	%	%
Private pension plans covering employees in private industry	27	30	39	18	24
Government pension plans covering federal, state and local government employees	36	37	31	62	36
Union pension plans	9	10	11	7	10
Social Security	15	12	12	5	14
None	1	1	1	—	1
Not sure	12	9	6	9	14

Table IV-7

LEAST PREFERRED SOURCE OF RETIREMENT INCOME
(Asked of current and retired employees)

Q.: Finally, which **one** of these sources would you **least** prefer to rely on for all your retirement income?

(Number of respondents)	Total Current And Retired Employees (1665)	Current Employees			
		Total (1308)	Covered By Private Plan (685)	Covered By Public Plan (229)	Not Covered (448)
	%	%	%	%	%
Private pension plans covering employees in private industry	11	11	11	11	11
Government pension plans covering federal, state and local government employees	4	4	5	1	3
Union pension plans	24	24	25	25	22
Social Security	37	43	44	52	37
None	1	1	1	*	1
Not sure	23	18	15	11	25

*Less than 0.5%.

Table IV-8

RETIREMENT INCOME SOURCE MOST IN NEED OF CHANGE
(Asked of current and retired employees)

Q.: And in general, which one is most in need of change for the better?

(Number of respondents)	Total Current And Retired Employees (1636)	Current Employees			
		Total (1281)	Covered By Private Plan (670)	Covered By Public Plan (225)	Not Covered (442)
	%	%	%	%	%
Private pension plans covering employees in private industry	9	9	9	9	9
Government pension plans covering federal, state and local government employees	6	6	6	8	6
Union pension plans	10	10	11	9	10
Social Security	53	59	60	63	54
None	1	*	*	—	1
Not sure	21	15	13	11	21

*Less than 0.5%.

Employee Satisfaction with Private Pension Plans

Both before and after passage of the Employee Retirement Income Security Act of 1974, private pension plans have been criticized for being financially unsound, for promising what they may not be able to deliver, and for various inequities in the way

43

employees become eligible for benefits. By and large, however, these views are not shared by people currently covered by private pension plans. Regardless of the criticisms leveled against private plans, employees are basically satisfied with the way their plans are designed and administered. At the same time, however, a small but significant minority have less than full confidence in the ability of their pension plan to pay the benefits due them when they retire. Only 6% have no confidence at all in their plan.

Observation:

These findings are clearly upbeat and should be read as positive marks for private pensions. But it is important to note here that the findings cannot be interpreted as a public sanction of the status quo in the private pension system. When employees say they are satisfied with their plan, many are not thinking about the benefits they will need during retirement and many do not know what benefits their plan will provide. As will be seen in a later chapter, employees feel it is extremely important that their plans contain provisions which are included in relatively few plans today, such as cost of living benefits and survivor benefits.

Table IV-9

SATISFACTION WITH DESIGN AND ADMINISTRATION OF PLAN
(Asked of those covered by a private pension plan)

Q.: How satisfied are you with the way your plan is designed and administered — very satisfied, somewhat satisfied, somewhat unsatisfied, or very unsatisfied?

(Number of respondents)	Total (595) %
Very satisfied	43
Somewhat satisfied	35
Somewhat unsatisfied	11
Very unsatisfied	5
Not sure	6

Business leaders have a generally accurate view of their employees' attitudes toward their plans. When asked how satisfied a majority of their employees would be about the design and administration of their plans, 59% of the leaders feel a majority of their employees would be very satisfied, 38% believe their employees would be somewhat satisfied, and only 3% feel their employees would be dissatisfied. Thus a majority of the leaders interviewed are correct in their assessment that a majority of their employees are satisfied with the way their plan is designed and administered.

Table IV-10

EMPLOYERS' PERCEPTIONS OF EMPLOYEES' SATISFACTION WITH PENSION PLAN DESIGN AND ADMINISTRATION
(Asked of business leaders)

Q.: And how satisfied would you say the majority of your employees are about the way their benefit plans are designed and administered — very satisfied, somewhat satisfied, somewhat dissatisfied, or very dissatisfied?

(Number of respondents)	Total (211)
	%
Very satisfied	59
Somewhat satisfied	38
Somewhat dissatisfied	3
Very dissatisfied	—
Not sure	—

Two out of three employees covered by private plans say they have a great deal of confidence that their plan will pay the benefits they are entitled to when they retire. Though this is a substantial majority, a significant percentage of employees voice some skepticism: 25% have "some confidence" that their plan will pay the benefits, and 6% have "hardly any confidence."

Business leaders are far more confident than employees that their plans will pay their promised benefits. Three percent have "some confidence," but an overwhelming 97% have "a great deal of confidence" that their plans will pay the benefits employees are entitled to when they retire.

Table IV-11

CONFIDENCE THAT PENSION PLAN WILL PAY BENEFITS
(Asked of current employees covered by private pension plan and of business leaders)

Q.: And how much confidence do you have that your pension plan will pay the benefits you are entitled to when you retire — a great deal of confidence, some confidence, or hardly any confidence at all?

Q.: How much confidence do you have that your pension plan will pay the benefits employees are entitled to when they retire — a great deal of confidence, some confidence, or hardly any confidence at all?

(Number of respondents)	Pension Plan Participants (593)	Total Business Leaders (211)
	%	%
Great deal of confidence	68	97
Some confidence	25	3
Hardly any confidence	6	—
Not sure	1	—

One of the major criticisms against company and union pensions is that they will not be able to pay employees all they have been promised. However, no evidence of this was found among current company or union pension plan beneficiaries. When asked whether they had ever been promised a benefit which they did not or were not going to receive, 93% replied that they had not, and 4% were not sure. Of the 7 people who said they had been promised a benefit they were not going to receive, 3 people later claimed that the benefits were actually forthcoming but had been delayed.

Table IV-12

WHETHER PROMISED BENEFIT NOT RECEIVED
(Asked of retired employees receiving company or union pension benefits)

Q.: Have you ever thought you had been promised a pension benefit that you now know you are never going to receive, or not?

(Number of respondents)	Total (169)
	%
Have been promised	4
Have not been promised	93
Not sure	4

Lastly, it is interesting to note that employers and employees have radically different views as to who owns the money in pension funds. Eight out of ten business leaders feel that employees own the money in their pension fund, but just more than 1 in 3 (36%) employees express the same view. A plurality (40%) of employees feel that their employer owns the money in their pension plan.

Table IV-13

OWNERSHIP OF MONEY IN PENSION FUND
(Asked of business leaders and those covered by a private pension plan)

Q.: As far as you are concerned, who owns the money in your [company's] pension fund — employees themselves, or your employer [the company] or union?

(Number of respondents)	Private Pension Plan Participating (592)	Total Business Leaders (208)
	%	%
Employees themselves	36	80
Employer/company	40	14
Union	9	2
Both (vol.)	11	4
Not applicable (vol.)	1	7
Not sure	6	1

CHAPTER V:

PENSION PLAN REPORTING

Interest In and Effectiveness Of Pension Plan Disclosure Statements

The findings in Chapter III demonstrate that many employees understand the basic provisions of their pension plan, but that just as many are relying on limited or inaccurate knowledge. In this chapter we will examine employees' interest in and reaction to various pension plan disclosure statements, along with their and business leaders' concerns about what types of information should be conveyed to employees.

More than 8 of 10 participants in private pension plans (83%) have received a report from their employer describing their plan and telling them what benefits they are entitled to; 15% say they have not received such a report. Thus a sizeable majority have received either a summary plan description or a personal benefits statement.

Most business leaders (78%) say employees covered by their company's pension plan automatically receive an annual personal benefits statement, while 22% say their employees do not automatically receive such a statement. Whether or not an employee will automatically receive a personal benefits statement varies with the size of the company, with the larger companies more likely to automatically distribute the reports.

Table V-1

WHETHER RECEIVED REPORT FROM EMPLOYER DESCRIBING BENEFITS OF PENSION PLAN
(Asked of those covered by a private pension plan)

Q.: Have you ever received a report from your employer describing your pension plan and telling you what **benefits** you are entitled to under your pension plan, or not?

(Number of respondents)	Total (595)
	%
Have received report	83
Have not received report	15
Not sure	2

Table V-2

WHETHER EMPLOYEES AUTOMATICALLY RECEIVE ANNUAL REPORT INDICATING RETIREMENT BENEFITS
(Asked of business leaders)

Q.: Do the employees covered by your company's pension plan also automatically receive a report or statement annually which indicates the benefits they as individuals will receive upon retirement, or don't they automatically receive such a report?

	Total Business Leaders (210)	Number Of Employees		
		2,000 or Less (62)	2,000 to 10,000 (65)	More than 10,000 (83)
(Number of respondents)	%	%	%	%
Do automatically receive	78	74	77	81
Do not automatically receive	22	26	23	19
Not sure	—	—	—	—

Of those who have ever received a report about their pension plan, 83% read the last report they received.

Most employers (76%) believe that between 76% and 100% of their employees who receive annual reports read them. They believe that summary plan descriptions are less widely read, with 46% estimating that one-fourth or less of their employees who receive them read them. Though employees were not asked directly about summary plan descriptions, other evidence suggests that they may well be less widely read than annual reports or personal benefits statements. For instance, the topics about which employees are least well-informed, such as vesting eligibility requirements, would be found in summary plan descriptions and not annual reports. A personal benefits statement usually mentions whether or not an employee is vested, but does not state the rules for this determination.

Table V-3

WHETHER READ LAST PENSION PLAN REPORT FROM EMPLOYER
(Asked of those who have received report)

Q.: Did you read the last report about your pension plan that you received from your employer, or not?

(Number of respondents)	Total (488) %
Read last report	83
Did not read last report	17
Not sure	*

*Less than 0.5%.

Table V-4

EMPLOYERS' ESTIMATE OF PERCENTAGE OF EMPLOYEES WHO READ ANNUAL REPORT
(Asked of those whose employees receive annual reports)

Q.: What percentage of those who receive the report or statement do you think actually read it?

(Number of respondents)	Total (164) %
None	—
1-25%	5
26-50%	4
51-75%	13
76-100%	76
Not sure	1
Mean percentage	72

Table V-5

EMPLOYERS' PERCEPTION OF PERCENTAGE OF EMPLOYEES
WHO READ THE SUMMARY PLAN DESCRIPTION
(Asked of business leaders)

Q.: Your employees automatically receive a summary plan description. About what percentage of those who receive the report do you think actually read it?

(Number of respondents)	Total (211)
	%
None	1
1-25%	46
26-50%	21
51-75%	13
76-100%	14
Not sure	4
Mean percentage	52

A substantial 88% of employees who read their last pension plan report claim they were able to understand what was in it, and only 10% were not. Wage workers are less likely to be able to understand the material in a pension report than salaried workers, though a still high 83% of those wage workers interviewed were able to understand the last report they read.

Most business leaders have an accurate perspective on their employees' ability to understand what is in a pension report. Sixty-seven percent (67%) of the leaders interviewed feel that more than three-quarters of their employees are able to understand most of what is in the report, and 85% think that more than half their employees can understand it. The summary plan description, containing more complex information, is believed to be less well-understood. Fifty-two percent (52%) of the leaders feel that half or less of their employees understand most of what is in the summary plan description, while 48% believe more than half understand it.

Table V-6

ABILITY TO UNDERSTAND PENSION PLAN REPORT
(Asked of those who have read last report)

Q.: Were you able to understand most of what was in the report, or not?

		Employment	
(Number of respondents)	Total (406)	Hourly Wage Worker (164)	Salaried (217)
	%	%	%
Able to understand	88	83	92
Not able to understand	10	15	6
Not sure	2	2	2

Table V-7

EMPLOYERS' ESTIMATE OF PERCENTAGE OF EMPLOYEES WHO UNDERSTAND
ANNUAL REPORT
(Asked of those whose employees receive annual report)

Q.: And what percentage of those who read the report or statement do you think are able to understand most of what is in it?

(Number of respondents)	Total (164) %
None	—
1-25%	4
26-50%	10
51-75%	18
76-100%	67
Not sure	—
Mean percentage	74

Table V-8

EMPLOYERS' PERCEPTIONS OF EMPLOYEES UNDERSTANDING OF
SUMMARY PLAN DESCRIPTIONS
(Asked of business leaders)

Q.: Generally, what percentage of those who read the summary plan description do you think are able to understand most of what is in it?

(Number of respondents)	Total (211) %
None	2
1-25%	30
26-50%	20
51-75%	17
76-100%	31
Not sure	1
Mean percentage	57

Helpfulness of Disclosure Statement

Nearly two-thirds (62%) of those who read the last pension plan report they received found it very helpful, and 33% found it somewhat helpful. Only 4% say the report was not helpful at all. Employers are somewhat more positive about the helpfulness of the report than are employees. Eighty percent (80%) of the leaders interviewed feel the report is very helpful for employees, 16% feel that it is somewhat helpful, and 4% feel it is not helpful at all.

Interestingly, employers themselves tacitly acknowledge that improvements can be made in the summary plan description. Only 44% of the leaders feel the summary plan description is very helpful for employees, and another 40% rate it somewhat helpful. Sixteen percent (16%) feel the summary plan description is not helpful at all.

Table V-9

HELPFULNESS OF REPORT IN DESCRIBING PENSION PLAN
(Asked of those who have read last report)

Q.: How helpful was the report in telling you what you want to know about your pension plan — very helpful, somewhat helpful, or not helpful at all?

(Number of respondents)	Total (407) %
Very helpful	62
Somewhat helpful	33
Not helpful at all	4
Not sure	*

*Less than 0.5%.

Table V-10

HELPFULNESS TO EMPLOYEES OF ANNUAL REPORT
(Asked of those whose employees receive report)

Q.: In terms of telling them what they want to know about their pension plan, how helpful is this report or statement for employees — very helpful, somewhat helpful, or not helpful at all?

(Number of respondents)	Total (166) %
Very helpful	80
Somewhat helpful	16
Not helpful at all	4
Not sure	1

Table V-11

EMPLOYERS' PERCEPTIONS OF
HELPFULNESS OF SUMMARY PLAN DESCRIPTION TO EMPLOYEES
(Asked of business leaders)

Q.: In terms of telling them what they want to know about their pension plan, how helpful do you think the summary is for your employees — very helpful, somewhat helpful, or not helpful at all?

(Number of respondents)	Total (211) %
Very helpful	44
Somewhat helpful	40
Not helpful at all	16
Not sure	—

The following table shows how widely pension plan reports are received, read, and understood among all plan participants along with how helpful they perceive the report to be.

While 83% claim to have received a report describing their pension plan, the combination of those who did not read the report and those who never received it means that just 69% of all pension plan participants read the last report about their pension plan. A total of 61% understood most of what was in the report. Lastly, the report was very or somewhat useful for 43% of plan participants.

Observation:

The results here are consistent with those in the section about employees' knowledge of pension plans. Many employees are knowledgeable about their plans, and substantial majorities claim to read the information that is available to them. For the most part, employers receive positive marks for the content of the reports. Among employees who read them, many find them understandable and helpful. This is not to say, of course, that the reports cannot be improved. One-third of those who read their last report offer an unexceptional "somewhat helpful" rating.

While report contents may be improved, particularly in regard to the summary plan description, the limiting factor in employee knowledge about pension plans is not the reports themselves but that many employees fail to read them. Increased emphasis on the importance of reading these disclosure statements and perhaps some alternate approaches to presenting the information, such as seminars, counseling, or audio-visual presentations, may help employees get a better understanding of their pension plan and develop a stronger sense of what they personally must do to be prepared for retirement.

Table V-12

SUMMARY OF PENSION PLAN DISCLOSURE FINDINGS
(Asked of employees covered by a private pension plan)

(Number of respondents)	Total (595) %
Total private pension plan participants who have:	
Received a report describing pension plan and telling what benefits they are entitled to	83
Read the report	69
Understood most of what was in the report	61
Found the report very or somewhat helpful	43

The Information Needs of Employees

Regardless of their level of knowledge about their pension plan, most employees feel strongly about being kept well-informed. Seventy-five percent (75%) say that it is very important they be informed about their pension plan, while 19% say it is somewhat important, and only 5% say it is not important at all. This 75% who feel it is very important to be informed about their pension plan roughly corresponds to the 69% who received and actually read their last pension plan report.

The importance of being kept informed about their pension plan is acknowledged by all employee groups whether wage worker, salaried, or self-employed.

Business leaders' attitudes on this question closely match those of their employees. Seventy-seven percent (77%) believe being kept informed about their pension plan is very important to employees, while 20% feel it is somewhat important, and 3% feel it is not important at all.

Table V-13

IMPORTANCE OF BEING KEPT INFORMED ABOUT PENSION PLAN
(Asked of those covered by a private pension plan)

Q.: How important is it to you that you be kept informed about your pension plan — very important, somewhat important, or not important at all?

		Employment		
(Number of respondents)	Total (594)	Hourly Wage Worker (268)	Salaried (289)	Self-Employed (29)
	%	%	%	%
Very important	75	75	75	71
Somewhat important	19	17	21	25
Not important at all	5	8	2	4
Not sure	1	—	1	—

Table V-14

EMPLOYER PERCEPTIONS OF IMPORTANCE OF KEEPING EMPLOYEES INFORMED ABOUT THEIR PENSION PLAN
(Asked of business leaders)

Q.: Among employees, do you think that being kept informed about their pension plan is very important, somewhat important, or not important at all?

(Number of respondents)	Total (211)
	%
Very important	77
Somewhat important	20
Not important at all	3
Not sure	—

Employees feel very strongly about the types of information they should receive about their pension plan.

An overwhelming 93% of those who read the last report think it is very important that they know how certain it is that they will be paid their pension on retirement. And more than 8 out of 10 feel it is very important that they know if their employer is making the necessary contributions to the plan, what their benefits will be upon retirement, whether or not they are vested, and what the current financial status is of the plan.

Though somewhat less important than the above, a substantial 6 out of 10 believe it is very important that they know where the pension funds are being invested, whether the company or the pension fund trustees or a professional management company is handling the investments, and what the return has been on investments.

Table V-15

IMPORTANCE OF VARIOUS KINDS OF INFORMATION IN REPORT
(Asked of those who have read last report)

Q.: How important is it that the report contain information about (ITEM) — very important, somewhat important, or not important at all?

(Number of respondents: 409)		Very Important	Somewhat Important	Not Important	Not Sure
How certain it is that you will really be paid your pension upon retirement	%	93	5	2	1
Whether your employer is making the necessary contributions to your pension plan	%	87	9	3	1
What the benefits are that you will receive upon your retirement	%	87	9	3	1
Whether you would be entitled to any benefits from your pension plan if you terminated work today	%	85	10	5	*
The current financial status of the plan	%	83	14	2	1
Where the pension funds are being invested	%	60	21	14	5
Whether the company, or the pension fund trustees, or a professional pension management company is handling the investments	%	60	23	12	4
What the return has been on investments	%	59	28	10	4

*Less than 0.5%.

Business Leader Attitudes Toward Employee Information Needs

Business leaders are sharply out of line with their employees as to what information should be reported about pension plans.

Business leaders share their employees' view about the importance of knowing what benefits they will receive when they retire. They also feel, though not as strongly as employees, that it is important for employees to know how certain it is that they will really be paid their pension benefits upon retirement, and whether or not they are vested.

But only 64% of employers, compared with 87% of employees, feel it is very important that employees know whether their company is making the necessary contributions to the pension plan. Only 38% feel it is very important that employees know the current financial status of the plan — a substantial 45 percentage point difference separating employers and employees on this point. Further, only 17% of business leaders feel it is important for their employees to know who is handling their pension investments, just 16% believe it is very important that employees know what the return has been on investments, and an even smaller 10% feel it is very important to know where the pension funds are being invested. These findings separate employers from employees by gaps of 43 points, 43 points, and 50 points respectively.

Table V-16

EMPLOYERS' PERCEPTIONS OF THE IMPORTANCE TO EMPLOYEES OF
VARIOUS KINDS OF INFORMATION IN REPORT
(Asked of business leaders whose employees receive annual report)

Q.: How important is it that the report or statement contain information for employees
about (ITEM) — very important, somewhat important, or not important at all?

(Number of respondents: 168)		Very Important	Somewhat Important	Not Important At All	Not Sure
What the benefits are that the employees will receive upon their retirement	%	93	6	1	1
How certain it is that employees will really be paid their pension upon retirement	%	84	5	10	1
Whether the employees would be entitled to any benefits from their pension plan if they terminated work today	%	76	21	4	—
Whether your company is making the necessary contributions to the pension plan	%	64	20	17	—
The current financial status of the plan	%	38	44	18	1
Whether the company, or the pension fund trustees, or a professional pension management company is handling the investments	%	17	46	37	—
What the return has been on investments	%	16	32	51	1
Where the pension funds are being invested	%	10	40	50	1

Employee Satisfaction With Pension Plan Information Currently Received

Though they have sharply divergent views from employers about the importance of various types of information, employees are generally favorable in their assessment of the information currently provided. In terms of telling them how certain it is that they will receive pension benefits on retirement, whether or not they are vested, and whether their employer is making the necessary contributions to the plan, approximately 8 of every 10 employees who read the last pension report give it a positive rating. Also, 80% give the report a positive rating for telling them what their personal benefits will be when they retire, and 81% have positive views toward the information about the current financial status of the plan.

Smaller but still substantial majorities are satisfied with information they receive about who is handling the pension investments, where the funds are being invested, and what the return has been on the investments.

Observation:

The findings in this section have an important implication for business leaders and pensions experts. Business leaders widely misjudge the importance employees place on certain types of information about their pension plans. For the most part, employees are satisfied with the types of information they currently receive, but the widely divergent views between employees and employers spell employee dissatisfaction for the future. Because some employees may seem uninterested in pensions, and some may not read or request pension information, this does not mean that the concerns of those who are interested can be taken lightly.

The findings suggest that business leaders should reassess their understanding of the information needs of their employees. The bulk of employees are very interested in their pension plan and are likely to become more so — with better articulated information needs — as they become more concerned with and move closer to their retirement period.

Table V-17

RATING OF REPORT ON PROVIDING VARIOUS KINDS OF INFORMATION
(Asked of those who have read last report)

Q.: And how would you rate the report in terms of telling you (ITEM) — is it excellent, pretty good, only fair, or poor?

(Number of respondents: 396)		Excellent	Pretty Good	Only Fair	Poor	Not Sure
How certain it is that you will really be paid your pension upon retirement	%	45	38	10	3	3
Whether you would be entitled to any benefits from your pension plan if you terminated work today	%	45	36	9	5	5
Whether your employer is making the necessary contributions to your pension plan	%	43	36	10	5	6
What the benefits are that you will receive upon your retirement	%	43	37	10	3	6
The current financial status of the plan	%	41	40	10	4	4
Whether the company, or the pension fund trustees, or a professional pension management company is handling the investments	%	36	31	12	7	14
Where the pension funds are being invested	%	35	28	13	12	11
What the return has been on investments	%	34	40	11	7	8

CHAPTER VI:

PENSION PLAN FUNDING

The Amount of Pension Plan Funding

Of many issues surrounding pension and pension plan reform, none has been more hotly debated than the question of funding and unfunded liabilities. This chapter will examine the business community's attitudes toward pension plan funding and toward the much-publicized question of unfunded pension liabilities. The findings here do not reveal the extent to which unfunded pension liabilities are or are not a problem — that is a task best left to pensions experts. But they do provide an objective assessment of business leaders' concerns about pension funding and their reactions to the problem of unfunded pension liabilities.

Certainly one of the reasons that pension funding has received so much public attention in recent times is that pension funds account for an enormous portion of the nation's investment capital. The amount of capital that currently backs the nation's private pension systems has grown rapidly in the past ten years, is presently in excess of $300 billion, and by one estimate is expected to grow by at least 11% per year to $1 trillion by the late 1980's.

Twenty-five percent (25%) of the business leaders interviewed in our sample are employed by companies having pension plans with less than $10 million in total assets, 28% by companies having between $10 and $69 million in assets, 25% by companies having between $70 and $249 million in assets, and 22% by companies having total pension fund assets of $250 million or more.

On average, the companies in our sample contributed an annual amount equal to 11.1% of their payroll costs. Company contributions to employees' pension plans as a percentage of total payroll costs vary only slightly with the size of the company, with larger companies contributing a slightly higher percentage.

Table VI-1

TOTAL ASSETS IN COMPANY'S PENSION PLAN
(Asked of business leaders)

Q.: What are the approximate total assets of your company's employee pension plans (including profit sharing and employee thrift plans)?

(Number of respondents)	Total (202) %
Less than $10 million	25
$10 million to $69 million	28
$70 million to $249 million	25
$250 million or more	22

Table VI-2

COMPANY'S ANNUAL PENSION PLAN CONTRIBUTION
(Asked of business leaders)

Q.: And what is your company's annual contribution to employee pension plans (including profit sharing and employee thrift plans), as a percentage of your total payroll costs?

(Number of respondents)	Total (193)	Number Of Employees		
		2,000 Or Less (54)	2,001 To 10,000 (61)	More Than 10,000 (78)
	%	%	%	%
1-2%	4	6	2	2
3-4%	6	11	—	8
5-6%	14	15	17	11
7-8%	16	13	21	16
9-10%	16	17	21	12
11-12%	9	8	10	11
13-14%	8	4	3	16
15-16%	11	8	17	9
17-18%	4	4	5	4
19-20%	6	9	3	7
21-22%	3	—	—	5
23-25%	2	2	—	1
More than 25%	3	2	2	1
Not sure	2	4	—	—
Mean percentage	11.1	9.8	10.5	11.5

The Adequacy of Funding

As most business executives see it, their company's pension plans are well or at least adequately funded. In terms of the benefits that have been promised, 69% claim their company's plan is well funded, 29% claim it is adequately funded, and only 2% say their plan is underfunded.

Smaller companies are considerably more likely to feel their pension plan is well funded than larger companies. Still, not less than 95% of the executives interviewed within any company size grouping feel their plan is at least adequately funded.

Business leaders are clearly concerned about unfunded vested pension liabilities, though, as will be seen in the following section, they are not particularly alarmed. The results here show that companies with relatively high proportions of liabilities that are unfunded are more concerned about the adequacy of their company's pension fund than companies with smaller or no unfunded liabilities. For instance, among companies with between 1% and 25% of total vested liabilities unfunded, 72% claim their funds are well funded, but among companies with more than 25% vested liabilities unfunded, just 34% make the same claim. At the same time, it should be noted that only 5% in this latter group feel their company's pension plan is underfunded.

Table VI-3

ADEQUACY OF PENSION PLAN'S FUNDING
(Asked of business leaders)

Q.: Let's talk about funding for a minute. Would you say that your company's pension plan is well funded, adequately funded, or somewhat underfunded, in terms of the benefits that have been promised?

(Number of respondents)	Total (210)	Number Of Employees			Unfunded Vested Liabilities		
		2,000 Or Less (61)	2,001 To 10,000 (65)	More Than 10,000 (84)	None (89)	1% To 25% (69)	More Than 25% (44)
	%	%	%	%	%	%	%
Well funded	69	82	58	67	83	72	34
Adequately funded	29	18	37	30	16	25	61
Underfunded	2	—	3	4	—	3	5
Not sure	*	—	2	—	1	—	—

*Less than 0.5%.

Unfunded Pension Liabilities

Fifty-six percent of the companies in our sample have some portion of their vested pension liabilities that is unfunded and 44% do not. Thirty-four percent of the firms have unfunded vested liabilities amounting to 25% or less of their total vested liabilities, 17% have unfunded vested liabilities of between 26% and 50% of total vested liabilities, and 4% have unfunded vested liabilities that account for more than half of their total vested liabilities.

Unfunded vested liabilities occur least frequently among smaller companies. Sixty-three percent of the firms interviewed with 2,000 employees or less report no unfunded vested liabilities, while the same claim is made by a smaller 41% of firms with between 2,000 and 10,000 employees, and 33% among firms with more than 10,000 employees. Also, the percentage of unfunded vested liabilities is lowest for companies whose total plan assets are less than $10 million, and second lowest among firms with relatively large pension funds of $250 million or more. The highest incidences of companies with unfunded vested pension liabilities, and of companies with the highest percentages of unfunded vested liabilities, are found among companies whose pension plan assets are in the middle range of between $10 and $249 million.

Table VI-4

PERCENTAGE OF COMPANY'S UNFUNDED VESTED PENSION LIABILITIES
(Asked of business leaders)

Q.: What percentage of your company's vested pension liabilities are unfunded?

(Number of respondents)	Total (203)	Number Of Employees			Pension Plan Assets			
		2,000 Or Less (60)	2,001 To 10,000 (63)	More Than 10,000 (80)	Less Than $10 Million (49)	$10 Million To $69 Million (55)	$70 Million To $249 Million (49)	$250 Million Or More (45)
	%	%	%	%	%	%	%	%
None	44	63	41	33	67	38	29	40
1-25%	34	22	37	41	24	35	39	42
26-50%	17	13	14	21	8	20	24	13
51-75%	2	2	2	4	—	2	6	2
76-100%	2	—	6	1	—	5	2	2

There is a considerable concern about unfunded pension liabilities within the business community. Unfunded pension liabilities — understood to be the accumulated costs of all prior service not yet funded — are believed to be a major problem afflicting private pensions in this country by 27% of the business leaders interviewed. Another 61% believe unfunded pension liabilities are a minor problem, and just 8% say they are not a problem at all.

More than anything, executives who feel unfunded pension liabilities are a major problem are concerned about the danger of future financial difficulties (13%) and that the benefits for employees are not secure (11%). More than 6 out of 10 executives feel that unfunded pension liabilities present only a minor problem. This is because, they feel, most pensions are adequately funded (28%), and the liability will be worked out in time (16%). Eleven percent feel the problem has been inflated. Finally, the consensus among those who do not view unfunded liabilities as a problem is that most pensions are currently adequately funded and that the liability will be worked out in time.

Table VI-5

WHETHER UNFUNDED PENSION LIABILITIES ARE A PROBLEM
(Asked of business leaders)

Q.: In the past few years, unfunded liabilities have received a considerable amount of attention. Generally, do you think unfunded pension liabilities are a major problem afflicting private pensions in this country today, a minor problem, or not at all?

(Number of respondents)	Total (212)
	%
A major problem	27
A minor problem	61
Not a problem at all	8
Not sure	3

Table VI-6

UNFUNDED PENSION LIABILITIES
(Asked of business leaders)

Q.: Why do you feel that unfunded pension liabilities are:

(Number of respondents: 212)	A Major Problem %	A Minor Problem %	No Problem At All %
Companies have obligations larger than assets	8	3	—
Danger of future financial difficulties	13	1	—
Benefits not secure, no guarantee employee will get benefits	11	4	—
Because of inflation	3	1	—
PBGC plan obligation	*	—	—
Most pensions are adequately funded	1	28	2
Liability will be worked out in time	—	16	3
ERISA/guarantee insurance lessens liability	*	6	1
Problem has been inflated	*	11	2
Amount of unfunded liabilities is not great	—	8	1
All other	—	—	—
Not sure	—	—	—

*Less than 0.5%.

More than half the leaders interviewed say unfunded pension liabilities are a concern for their company. Unfunded pension liabilities are a major concern for 16% of the companies included in the sample, a minor concern for 38%, and not a concern at all for 45%.

Predictably, the larger a company's unfunded vested liability, measured as a percentage of total vested liabilities, the greater the concern about unfunded liabilities. A sizeable 40% of those in firms with more than 25% vested liabilities unfunded say that such liabilities are a major concern. Unfunded liabilities are a minor concern to another 42% of the executives in this grouping. Interestingly, even among companies that claim to have no unfunded vested liabilities, 30% are somewhat concerned about the unfunded liability problem.

Observation:

A company's ability to meet its future pension obligations and the significance of the unfunded liability problem are extremely complex issues that rest on a number of economic contingencies and actuarial assumptions, and which lie beyond the scope of this report. However, it is clear that unfunded pension liabilties are a problem of some concern to the American business community. Business leaders are not alarmed — many feel the problem has been overblown and that the liabilities will be reduced by better investment performance and amortization over a number of years. But a sizeable percentage are worried about the effects of unfunded pension liabilities upon their own company.

If anything, the results point to a stark inconsistency between what the media implies is a seemingly imminent crisis facing pension plan beneficiaries and the more restrained views of the business community. It behooves pensions experts, government regulators, and the business community to further examine the perceived problems associated with unfunded pension liabilities, and to provide a clearer perspective on what effect those perceived problems may have on the financial stability of American business and the economic security of future retirees.

Table VI-7

CONCERN TO COMPANY WITH UNFUNDED PENSION LIABILITIES
(Asked of business leaders)

Q.: Would you say that unfunded pension liabilities are a major concern for your company, a minor concern, or not a concern at all?

(Number of respondents)	Total (211)	Unfunded Vested Liabilities		
		None (90)	1% To 25% (69)	More Than 25% (43)
	%	%	%	%
Major concern	16	7	13	40
Minor concern	38	23	54	42
Not a concern	45	68	33	19
Not sure	1	2	—	—

Attitudes Toward Socially Desirable Investment Policies

Another concern that has received considerable public attention recently has been the question of whether or not pension funds should be invested to achieve political or social goals as well as economic goals.

By 66-19%, business leaders feel pension funds should be invested wherever they bring the largest return, regardless of the social policies of the companies or countries in which they might be invested.

Employees covered by private pension plans are nearly evenly split on the issue. This question was asked of pension plan participants in two stages. First, they were asked, "Which do you think — that pension funds should not be invested in companies or countries with socially undesirable policies, or funds should be invested wherever they bring the largest return?" In response, 41% favor investing funds wherever they bring the largest return, while a 47% plurality feel that funds should not be invested in companies or countries with socially undesirable policies.

Next, respondents who felt pension funds should not be invested in certain companies or countries were asked whether they would still favor withholding such investments if it meant a lower return on the investments, which would in turn mean lower pension benefits for them. Here a surprisingly high 84% claim they would still favor withholding investments from socially undesirable companies or countries, and only 9% alter their view, with 6% not sure. This leaves a total of 38% who support socially desirable funding policies, and 45% who feel funds should be invested wherever they bring the largest return.

Observation:

The question of socially desirable funding policies is a latent but potentially powerful issue that may become more publicly salient in the future. A substantial minority of those covered by private pensions — people likely to be hurt by poor investment performance — are strongly opposed to investing pension funds in companies or countries with socially unde-

sirable policies. Even if it meant lower benefits for them, the overwhelming majority of this group would still favor withholding investments from certain companies or countries. Though it is unlikely that there will be across-the-board demands for socially desirable funding policies, business leaders should not be surprised to encounter sporadic instances of stiff opposition to investing in companies or countries whose policies are particularly antithetical to various subgroups in the population.

Table VI-8

WHETHER PENSION FUNDS SHOULD BE INVESTED IN COMPANIES OR COUNTRIES WITH SOCIALLY UNDESIRABLE POLICIES
(Asked of employees covered by private pension plans and of business leaders)

Q.: Some people feel that pension funds should not be invested in companies or countries that practice certain types of socially undesirable policies, like Rhodesia. Others feel that pension funds should be invested wherever they will bring the largest return, regardless of the policies of the companies or countries. Which do you think — that pension funds should not be invested in companies or countries with socially undesirable policies, or funds should be invested wherever they bring the largest return?

Q.: How do you feel about where pension funds should be invested — that pension funds should be invested wherever they bring the largest return, or that funds should **not** be invested in companies or countries with socially undesirable policies?

(Number of respondents)	Private Pension Plan Participants (593)	Total Business Leaders (207)
	%	%
Fund should not be invested in companies/countries with socially undesirable policies	47	19
Funds should be invested wherever they bring the largest return	41	66
Not sure	12	15

Table VI-9

WHETHER FAVOR WITHHOLDING INVESTMENT FROM CERTAIN COMPANIES OR COUNTRIES IF WOULD RESULT IN LOWER BENEFITS
(Asked of employees who believe funds should not be invested in companies or countries with socially undesirable policies)

Q.: Suppose not investing in certain companies or countries meant there would be a lower return on investments that could mean lower benefits to you. In this case, would you still favor withholding investments from certain companies or countries, or not?

(Number of respondents)	Total (270)
	%
Would still favor withholding investments	84
Would not still favor withholding investments	9
Not sure	6

CHAPTER VII:

PRIVATE PENSIONS: SOME POLICY CONSIDERATIONS

Employees' and Retirees' Attitudes on Characteristics of Pension Plans

Current and retired employees have some strong ideas about the importance of various features of a pension plan. So too does the business community, and more often than not the two groups have notably different views.

Respondents were asked about the importance of several characteristics of pension plans, including survivor benefits, portability, the right to receive vested benefits, benefit guarantees, the provision of enough income to maintain an acceptable standard of living after retirement, and the provision of benefits that go up with the cost of living.

To current and retired employees, by far the most important of these characteristics is that the plan have benefits that go up with the cost of living. A significant 66% list this pension plan characteristic as extremely important, and another 27% call it very important. Current and retired employees are also deeply concerned about being able to receive the benefits for which they are eligible, regardless of pension fund investment performance. Sixty-one percent feel this is an extremely important characteristic to have in their plan. Also high on the list is the provision of survivor benefits, mentioned as extremely important by 56% of those interviewed. Other features are of less, but still considerable, importance to people in the group. They would prefer a plan that provides enough money for them to maintain the same standard of living as before retirement (47% extremely important), a plan that permits them to collect vested benefits if they leave work before retirement (43%), and a plan that permits them to transfer accrued benefits to another pension plan if they change employers (39%).

When asked which two or three of these features are most important to have in their plan, current and retired employees most frequently mention cost of living benefits (58%) and the provision of enough money to maintain a pre-retirement standard of living (46%), followed by survivor benefits (38%) and benefits that are guaranteed regardless of fund investment performance (33%).

Demands for pension benefits that increase with inflation and the cost of living are likely to get stronger and louder in the future. Among retirees who receive company or union pension benefits, just 30% say they have received cost of living increases and 66% say they have not. Moreover, among those who receive cost of living benefits, nearly one-third (30%) received their last cost of living increase between one and five years ago.

Observation:

In actuality, private pension plans with cost of living provisions are relatively rare, and the 30% of private plan beneficiaries who claim their plan contains such a provision is somewhat suspicious (Table VII-3). It seems most likely that many respondents on the question were referring to ad hoc adjustments they have received in their benefit check, rather than provisions for regular cost of living increases.

Table VII-I

IMPORTANCE OF VARIOUS PENSION PLAN CHARACTERISTICS
(Asked of current and retired employees)

Q.: I'm going to read several characteristics of pension plans. For each, please tell me how important you think it is that a pension plan have that characteristic — extremely important, very important, only somewhat important, or not important at all.

(Number of respondents: 1691)	Extremely Important	Very Important	Somewhat Important	Not Important	Not Sure
	%	%	%	%	%
That your pension benefits will go up as the cost of living goes up	66	27	5	1	1
That you are guaranteed to receive the pension benefits you are eligible for, regardless of what happens to the pension fund investments made over the years you have been working	61	31	4	1	3
That your pension provides survivor benefits for your spouse in case you die	56	27	7	7	2
That your pension provides enough money for you to maintain the same standard of living as before your retirement	47	37	13	3	1
Once you have qualified for some pension benefits with a particular employer, that you are able to collect these benefits when you retire, even if you work for another employer before retirement	43	36	11	5	5
Once you have qualified for some pension benefits with a particular employer, that you are able to transfer those benefits to another pension plan if you change employers	39	35	13	8	5
That your pension provides less money than when you worked, but enough for you to maintain an acceptable standard of living	32	40	17	6	5

Table VII-2

MOST IMPORTANT PENSION PLAN CHARACTERISTICS
(Asked of current and retired employees)

Q.: And which two or three of these characteristics I've just read would you say are the most important to have in your pension plan?

(Number of respondents)	Total (1536) %
That your pension benefits will go up as the cost of living goes up	58
That your pension provides enough money for you to maintain the same standard of living as before your retirement	46
That your pension provides survivor benefits for your spouse in case you die	38
That you are guaranteed to receive the pension benefits you are eligible for, regardless of what happens to the pension fund investments made over the years you have been working	33
That your pension provides less money than when you worked, but enough for you to maintain an acceptable standard of living	16
Once you have qualified for some pension benefits with a particular employer, that you are able to collect those benefits when you retire, even if you work for another employer before retirement	16
Once you have qualified for some pension benefits with a particular employer, that you are able to transfer those benefits to another pension plan if you change employers	15
None	*
Not sure	2

*Less than 0.5%.

Table VII-3

WHETHER PENSION HAS COST-OF-LIVING INCREASE PROVISION*
(Asked of retired employees receiving company or union pension benefits)

Q.: Does your pension have a provision to have the benefits increase as the cost of living increases, or not?

(Number of respondents)	Total (169) %
Has provision	30
Does not have provision	66
Not sure	4

*The high percentage claiming their plan has a cost of living provision seems unlikely. We assume that many respondents are referring to ad hoc adjustments.

Table VII-4

TIME OF LAST INCREASE
(Asked of retired employees who have received an increase from
company or union plan)

Q.: When was the last time you received an increase — within the last 6 months, 6 months
to a year ago, 1 to 5 years ago, or more than 5 years ago?

(Number of respondents)	Total (51)
	%
Within the last 6 months	33
6 months to 1 year ago	30
1 to 5 years ago	30
More than 5 years ago	3
Not sure	—

Business Leaders' Attitudes on Desirable Characteristics of Pension Plans

Business leaders consider cost of living benefits to be far less important than do
current and former employees. Only 13% of the leaders feel that having pension benefits
that go up as the cost of living goes up is an extremely important characteristic of a
pension plan. Thirty-eight percent rate this characteristic very important, but a sizeable
47% say it is either only somewhat important or not important at all. Also, while this
feature ranks 1st in importance among the employee group, it ranks only 5th among
business leaders.

The leaders interviewed feel it is important that an employee be guaranteed the
benefits he is eligible for regardless of investment performance (46% extremely important),
and that once the employee has qualified for benefits, he will be able to collect them when
he retires even if he has changed jobs before retirement (46%).

Somewhat surprisingly, business leaders share the employee concerns about survivor benefits, rated extremely important by 43% of those interviewed. But business
leaders and current and retired employees are again at odds on the question of the amount
of money that should be provided through a pension. Business leaders would prefer
that a pension provide less money to a retiree than when he worked, but enough for him
to maintain an acceptable standard of living (35%). However, the employee and retiree
group would prefer that a pension provide enough money for the retiree to maintain the
same standard of living as before retirement, a feature that is listed as extremely important
by only 11% of the business leaders interviewed.

Lastly, portability has a relatively low priority among current and retired employees,
though it is felt to be extremely important by a substantial minority (39%). It also receives
a low priority in the business community, where it is perceived to be extremely important
by a significantly lower 8%.

Observation:

*It is interesting to note that most business leaders feel it is important for
a pension plan to have a provision for survivor benefits. Making such a
provision mandatory is currently under consideration by Congress as part
of the proposed ERISA Improvements Act. It should of course be realized
that believing in the importance of a provision and supporting its passage*

as a mandatory part of a pension plan are two entirely different matters, and the results here simply do not permit an assessment of business's position on the matter. As for employees, it is clear that they feel survivor benefits are a matter of great importance.

The most important issue for employees, however, is the problem of inflation. As it is currently planned, the ERISA Improvements Act does not deal with inflation or address employee demands for benefits that increase with inflation and the cost of living. Yet the problem is not going to go away; in fact, it is likely to become the number-one source of difficulties for pensions in the years ahead. Business leaders are also deeply concerned about inflation. Though they claim that cost of living benefits are relatively unimportant features of pension plans, this is not because they feel they are unimportant per se. Rather, they are worried about the costs that cost of living benefits would entail.

Unless the public debate is turned more directly to the problem and unless efforts are taken to help future retirees successfully combat inflation, the problems being addressed by the ERISA Improvements Act will seem small compared to what lies ahead.

Table VII-5

BUSINESS LEADERS' PERCEPTIONS
OF IMPORTANCE OF VARIOUS CHARACTERISTICS OF PENSION PLANS
(Asked of business leaders)

Q.: I'm going to read several characteristics of **pension plans**. For each, please tell me how important you think it is that a pension plan have that characteristic — extremely important, very important, only somewhat important, or not important at all.

(Number of respondents: 212)		Extremely Important	Very Important	Only Somewhat Important	Not Important	Not Sure
That the employee is guaranteed to receive the pension benefits he is eligible for, regardless of what happens to the pension fund investments made over the years he has been working	%	46	40	7	3	3
Once the employee has qualified for some pension benefits with a particular employer, that he is able to collect those benefits when he retires even if he works for another employer before retirement	%	46	38	12	4	1
That the pension provides survivor benefits for the employee's spouse in case he dies	%	43	40	16	1	1
That the pension provides less money to the retiree than when he worked, but enough for him to maintain an acceptable standard of living	%	35	55	8	1	1
That the pension benefits will go up as the cost of living goes up	%	13	38	37	10	2
That the pension provides enough money for the retiree to maintain the same standard of living as before his retirement	%	11	47	36	4	1
Once the employee has qualified for some pension benefits with a particular employer, that he is able to transfer those benefits to another pension plan if he changes employers	%	8	14	21	55	2

Calculating and Distributing Retirement Income

Findings throughout this survey show that there is a small but substantial minority of current and retired employees who feel that retirement income should be based on an individual's need, regardless of how much he or she made before retirement. When asked directly, 28% of the current and retired employees and 5% of business leaders believe that retirement income should be based on need. However, 58% of the public and an overwhelming 90% of business leaders feel that retirement income should be based on the amount of money made and the amount of time worked before retirement.

Table VII-6

PREFERENCES FOR RETIREMENT INCOME ELIGIBILITY REQUIREMENTS
(Asked of current and retired employees and of business leaders)

Q.: When someone retires, do you think their retirement income should be based on the amount of money they made and how long they worked before retirement, or on their need, regardless of how much they made before retirement?

(Number of respondents)	Total Current And Retired Employees (1694)	Total Business Leaders (210)
	%	%
On the amount of money made and how long they worked before retirement	58	90
On need, regardless of money made before retirement	28	5
On both	9	5
Not sure	5	*

*Less than 0.5%.

In terms of plan design, current and retired employees would prefer a plan that gave an adequate amount of money to a smaller number of people who have longer service with an employer (48%) rather than one that gave a small amount of money to as many people as possible (27%). Business leaders feel even more strongly in this regard, with 79% preferring to give an adequate amount of money to a smaller number with longer service.

Observation:

Interestingly, ERISA was based on the premise that it is better to give a small amount of money to many people rather than a larger amount to a smaller number of people. Mandatory participation, vesting, and funding schedules embodied in ERISA tend to divide a company's contribution among a greater number of people. Rightly or wrongly, Congress moved in the opposite direction to the views of the public in this respect.

Table VII-7

PREFERRED DESIGN OF PENSION PLAN
(Asked of current and retired employees and business leaders)

Q.: In terms of government policy toward pension plans, do you think pensions should be designed to give a small amount of money to as many people as possible, or to give an adequate amount of money to a smaller number of people who have longer service with an employer?

(Number of respondents)	Total Current And Retired Employees (1659)	Total Business Leaders (209)
	%	%
Give a small amount to many	27	6
Give an adequate amount to a smaller number who have longer service	48	79
It depends	15	12
Not sure	11	2

When it comes to the trade-off between small pension benefits that are guaranteed and larger benefits which are not guaranteed, both current and retired employees and business leaders would opt for a plan with guaranteed but small benefits.

By 75-6%, current and retired employees say they would rather have a pension plan that provides smaller benefits they are guaranteed to get, rather than a plan with larger benefits that are not guaranteed. Fifty percent of the leaders interviewed have an accurate understanding of their employees' preferences in this regard, while 33% feel that a majority of their employees would prefer a plan with larger, unguaranteed benefits.

A plan with small, guaranteed benefits is also the type of plan preferred by business leaders for their company. Fifty-two percent say they would prefer such a plan, compared with 27% who would prefer a plan having larger unguaranteed benefits. Preferences for plans with small, guaranteed benefits are strongest among smaller firms, though nearly half the leaders interviewed would prefer such plans, regardless of the number of workers employed by their firm.

Table VII-8

PREFERENCE FOR PLAN WITH GUARANTEED SMALL BENEFITS
OR UNGUARANTEED LARGER BENEFITS
(Asked of current and retired employees and of business leaders)

Q.: And would you rather have a pension plan that provides small benefits that you are guaranteed to get, or a plan that provides larger benefits that you are not guaranteed to get?

Q.: Which do you think a majority of your employees would prefer — a plan with guaranteed small benefits, or a plan with non-guaranteed larger benefits?

(Number of respondents)	Total Current And Retired Employees (1685)	Total Business Leaders (212)
	%	%
Small benefits	75	50
Larger benefits	6	33
It depends (vol.)	8	7
Neither (vol.)	7	5
Not sure	4	5

Table VII-9

PREFERENCE BETWEEN PENSION PLAN THAT GUARANTEES SMALL BENEFITS
OR LARGER BENEFITS NOT GUARANTEED
(Asked of business leaders)

Q.: And would you rather have a pension plan for your company that provides small benefits that employees are guaranteed to get, or a plan that provides larger benefits that employees are not guaranteed to get?

(Number of respondents)	Total (211)	Number Of Employees		
		2,000 Or Less (62)	2,001 To 10,000 (65)	More Than 10,000 (84)
	%	%	%	%
Small benefits	52	56	54	48
Larger benefits	27	19	25	33
It depends (vol.)	7	6	8	6
Neither (vol.)	12	16	11	11
Not sure	2	2	3	2

Integrated Benefit Formulas

Integrated benefit formulas, by which the amount a person will receive from Social Security is taken into account when determining the size of his pension benefits, are met with opposing views by business leaders and current and retired employees. By 77-22%, a majority of business leaders feel that Social Security benefits should be taken into account when determining the size of a pension benefit. But by 55-37%, a majority of current and retired employees believe that Social Security benefits should not be taken into account. This view is held more strongly by those covered by private and public pension plans.

Table VII-10

ATTITUDES TOWARD INTEGRATED BENEFIT FORMULAS
(Asked of current and retired employees and of business leaders)

Q.: When the size of the benefit that a person will receive from a pension plan is being determined, do you think the amount they will receive from Social Security should be taken into account or not?

(Number of respondents)	Total Current And Retired Employees (1690)	Pension Plan Coverage			Total Business Leaders (212)
		Private Plan (692)	Public Plan (230)	Not Covered (457)	
	%	%	%	%	%
Should be taken into account	37	35	28	39	77
Should not	55	60	67	53	22
Not sure	8	5	5	7	1

Portability

Today's employees have mixed views as to how their pension benefits should be handled if they change jobs before retirement, but they clearly do not favor transferring their benefits to a government held account. A narrow 34% plurality feel that their accrued benefits should be kept in their original pension plan and the benefits paid out when they retire. Thirty-one percent would prefer that the money be transferred to a separate account of their own, like an IRA, and paid to them when they retire. An almost equal 29% would prefer that the money be transferred to their new pension plan.

Though employees split almost evenly on these three proposals, they are virtually unanimous in their lack of support for the idea of having their benefits held by the federal government until their retirement. Only 2% indicate a preference for this proposal.

A greater consensus exists among the business community, where 72% would prefer that the money be kept in the original pension plan and paid out when the employee eventually retires. Generally speaking, the greater the assets in a company's pension plan, the more likely the company is to prefer this alternative. Among firms with pension plans of less than $10 million in total assets, a small but substantial minority (27%) would prefer that the pension benefits for an employee who leaves work before retirement be transferred to an account of his own like an IRA. Still, a 55% majority of those with under $10 million in total pension plan assets would prefer that the money be kept in the original plan.

72

Table VII-11

PREFERRED MEANS OF MAINTAINING BENEFITS IF CHANGE JOBS
(Asked of business leaders and those covered by private pension plans)

Q.: When you change jobs, there are several possible ways to maintain the pension benefits you have earned. Which one of the ways on this card would you **prefer** to be used to maintain your benefits if you change jobs?

Q.: As you know, when employees change jobs, there are several possible ways to maintain the pension benefits they have earned. Which one of the ways on this card would you prefer to be used to maintain employees' benefits if they change jobs?

(Number of respondents)	Current Employees Covered By Pension Plan (588)	Business Leaders				
				Pension Plan Assets		
		Total (209)	Less Than $10 Million (49)	$10 Million To $69 Million (56)	$70 Million To $249 Million (50)	$250 Million Or More (45)
	%	%	%	%	%	%
The money should be kept in my original pension plan and the benefits paid out when I retire	34	72	55	75	76	80
The money should be transferred to a separate account of my own, like an Individual Retirement Account, paid to me when I retire	31	14	27	13	10	9
The money should be transferred to my new pension plan	29	11	12	11	12	7
The money should be transferred to the federal government until I retire	2	1	2	—	—	2
Not sure	5	2	4	2	2	2

Contributions and Individual Retirement Accounts

Current and retired employees were asked whether they would favor a change in the pension law that would permit employees to contribute to pension plans at work and deduct their contributions from federal taxes until they retire. Nearly half (49%) would favor such a change in the pension law while 28% disapprove of the change. Seventeen percent are not sure.

The proposal receives strong support in the business community, where 89% say they would approve of a law permitting tax-deductible employee contributions to pension plans at work. One of the concerns of lawmakers considering this proposal is that the employer might use the law as a way to reduce his own contribution to the employee's pension plan. But by 75-23%, the business leaders interviewed do not favor making such employee contributions mandatory. Thus, most employers do not see the law as a way to reduce their own contributions to employee pension plans.

Table VII-12

APPROVAL OF LAW PERMITTING EMPLOYEE CONTRIBUTION TO PENSION PLANS
(Asked of current and retired employees)

Q.: Right now Congress is considering new laws that would permit employees to contribute to pension plans at work and deduct their contribution from federal taxes until they retire. The advantage of this measure is that it would permit employees to save more for retirement than they are saving now without paying full taxes on the money. The disadvantage is that the employer might expect the employee to pay more than he is paying now, so that the employer can reduce his own contribution. In general, would you approve or disapprove of such a law?

(Number of respondents)	Total (1687)
	%
Approve	49
Disapprove	28
Neither	6
Not sure	17

Table VII-13

BUSINESS LEADERS' ATTITUDES TOWARD PLAN TO PERMIT EMPLOYEES TO DEDUCT CONTRIBUTIONS TO PENSION PLAN FROM INCOME TAX
(Asked of business leaders)

Q.: Right now Congress is considering new laws that would permit employees to contribute to pension plans at work and deduct their contribution from federal taxes until they retire. In general, would you approve or disapprove of such a law?

(Number of respondents)	Total (212)
	%
Approve	89
Disapprove	11
Not sure	*

*Less than 0.5%.

Table VII-14

BUSINESS LEADERS' ATTITUDES TOWARD MANDATORY EMPLOYEE CONTRIBUTIONS TO PENSION PLAN
(Asked of business leaders)

Q.: If such deductions were permitted would you favor making employees' contribution **mandatory** to help cover the cost of providing pension benefits or not?

(Number of respondents)	Total (211)
	%
Would favor	23
Would not favor	75
Not sure	2

Another piece of legislation being considered would permit employees who are covered by a company or union pension plan to also put the money into their own Individual Retirement Account. The money would be exempt from taxes until retirement.

Such a change in the pension law would be welcomed by current pension plan participants. Thirty-one percent of those currently covered by a private pension plan say they would be very likely to contribute to their own retirement account and another 29% would be somewhat likely to do so. Thirty-one percent say they would be unlikely to open a retirement account in addition to their company pension.

The law would also be welcomed in the business community. Eighty-eight percent of the leaders interviewed say they would approve of such a law while only 9% would disapprove.

Observation:

Both the business community and employees are strongly in favor of employee contributions to pension plans. These include contributions to company plans at work and contributions to individual plans in addition to the employees' company plans. Permitting such contributions would seem to be an excellent way of helping today's employees fight the financial pressures they will face when they retire.

Table VII-15

LIKELIHOOD OF OPENING PERSONAL RETIREMENT ACCOUNT IN ADDITION TO EMPLOYER OR UNION PLAN
(Asked of current employees covered by private pension plan)

Q.: Suppose the pension law were changed, and in addition to your employer or union pension plan, you would be able to put some of your income into your own retirement account. You would pay no taxes on the money that you contribute but you would pay taxes on the money you would receive after you retire. If the pension law were changed in this way, how likely would you be to open your own retirement account — very likely, somewhat likely, somewhat unlikely, or very unlikely?

(Number of respondents)	Pension Plan Participants Total (592)
	%
Very likely	31
Somewhat likely	29
Somewhat unlikely	12
Very unlikely	19
It depends	4
Not sure	5

Table VII-16

BUSINESS LEADERS' ATTITUDES TOWARD PERMITTING BOTH PENSIONS AND TAX SHELTERED IRAs
(Asked of business leaders)

Q.: Suppose the pension law were changed and, in addition to their employer or union pension plan, employees would be able to put some of their income into their own retirement account. They would pay no taxes on the money that they contribute but would pay taxes on the money they would receive after retirement. In general, would you approve or disapprove of such a change in the pension law?

(Number of respondents)	Total (212)
	%
Approve	88
Disapprove	9
It depends (vol.)	3
Not sure	*

*Less than 0.5%.

Private Pensions: Defined Benefit or Defined Contribution

After hearing a description of a defined benefit plan and a defined contribution plan, current and retired employees were asked to rate the plans and indicate which they would prefer to be covered by. In looking at the following tables, it should be understood that the results indicate little more than their initial reaction to the various advantages and disadvantages of each plan and are not strongly held attitudes. Concepts such as defined benefit plan and defined contribution plan are complex and relatively unknown to the public, and one cannot expect to receive a well-thought-out response. Nevertheless, the results do provide a useful assessment of the gut reactions of current and retired employees to each funding formula.

After hearing the advantages and disadvantages of both types of plans, respondents are more favorably inclined toward defined benefit plans than defined contribution plans. Defined benefit plans receive a 49-41% positive rating, while defined contribution plans receive a 51-38% negative rating. And by 45-33% the working public and retirees in the sample would prefer to have a defined benefit plan over a defined contribution plan.

Table VII-17

RATING OF "DEFINED BENEFIT PLAN"
(Asked of current and retired employees)

Q.: There are several ways that employers can provide retirement income to their employees. In one of the ways, called a "**defined benefit plan**," the benefit that employees will get when they retire is set in advance, and the employer uses statistical estimates to determine how much to contribute to the pension fund each year. The advantage of this plan is that the employees know how much, in dollars, they are going to receive when they retire regardless of investment losses. The disadvantage is that the employee does not get any additional benefits from good investment results. In general, how does this type of plan sound to you — excellent, pretty good, only fair or poor?

(Number of respondents)	Total (1690)
	%
Excellent	9
Pretty good	39
Only fair	32
Poor	9
Not sure	10
Positive	49
Negative	41

Table VII-18

RATING OF "DEFINED CONTRIBUTION PLAN"
(Asked of current and retired employees)

Q.: In another type of plan, called a "**defined contribution plan**," the employer's yearly contribution to the pension fund is set in advance as a percentage of the employee's pay. The employer puts the money into an individual account for the employee, and when the employee retires he receives all the money in the account including investment results. The advantage of this plan is that the employee has a separate account of his own, and he can benefit from good investment results. The disadvantage is that the investment results may be poor, or the benefits are likely to be smaller than in other plans, because if an employee's salary is small when he first starts working, or if he enters the plan at an older age, only a small contribution will be made to the account. In general, how does this type of plan sound to you — excellent, pretty good, only fair or poor?

(Number of respondents)	Total (1690)
	%
Excellent	6
Pretty good	33
Only fair	38
Poor	13
Not sure	10
Positive	38
Negative	51

Table VII-19

WHETHER PREFER "DEFINED BENEFIT PLAN"
OR "DEFINED CONTRIBUTION PLAN"
(Asked of current and retired employees)

Q.: Now, of the two plans I have read — the defined benefit plan and the defined contribution plan — which type of plan would you personally prefer to have?

(Number of respondents)	Total (1688)
	%
Defined benefit plan	45
Defined contribution plan	33
Neither	9
Not sure	14

Employers feel much more strongly than employees about the advantages of defined benefit plans for employees. By 73-15%, employers feel that a defined benefit plan is better for employees than a defined contribution plan.

However, employers are not quite as certain about which type of plan is better for their company. Forty-nine percent feel a defined benefit plan would be best for their company, while 41% have the same view about defined contribution plans.

Table VII-20

WHETHER A DEFINED BENEFIT PLAN OR A DEFINED CONTRIBUTION PLAN
IS BETTER FOR EMPLOYEES
(Asked of business leaders)

Q.: What type of plan is better for employees — a defined benefit plan or a defined contribution plan?

(Number of respondents)	Total (211)
	%
Defined benefit	73
Defined contribution	15
Neither (vol.)	2
Not sure	9

Table VII-21

WHETHER A DEFINED BENEFIT PLAN OR A DEFINED CONTRIBUTION PLAN
IS BETTER FOR COMPANY
(Asked of business leaders)

Q.: And which is better for your company — a defined benefit or a defined contribution plan?

		Number Of Employees		
(Number of respondents)	Total (208)	2,000 Or Less (61)	2,001 To 10,000 (64)	More Than 10,000 (83)
	%	%	%	%
Defined benefit	49	51	44	52
Defined contribution	41	33	48	42
Neither (vol.)	2	3	—	4
Not sure	7	13	8	2

CHAPTER VIII:

EMPLOYEE CONTRIBUTIONS TO PENSION PLANS

Business Leader Outlook on Pension Costs

Inflation, demands for increased benefits, poor investment performance — all these are factors that are sure to push up pension costs in the future. Two out of every three executives interviewed say there is a strong possibility that their pension costs will increase as a percentage of pay in the future.

Regardless of the size of their firm, well more than half the business leaders feel there is a strong possibility of increased pension costs in the future. However, the chances for an increase in pension costs are highest among the largest firms, among whom 70% cite a strong possibility of increasing costs as a percentage of pay. It should be noted here that on average, the firms in the sample contribute an annual amount equal to 11.1% of payroll costs.

Part of the concern among business leaders about unfunded liabilities is fueled by the understanding that, barring dramatically improved investment results, pension costs will have to increase if liabilities are to decrease. Three out of every four leaders whose firms have more than 25% vested liabilities unfunded say there is a strong possibility of an increase in pension costs. A smaller but still substantial 58% say there is a strong possibility of increased costs among those whose pension funds have no unfunded vested liabilities.

Table VIII-1

POSSIBILITY OF PENSION COSTS INCREASING
AS A PERCENTAGE OF PAY
(Asked of business leaders)

Q.: What is the possibility that your pension costs will increase as a percentage of pay in the future — a strong possibility, a slight possibility, or no possibility at all?

		Number of Employees			Unfunded Vested Liabilities		
(Number of respondents)	Total (210)	2,000 Or Less (61)	2,001 To 10,000 (65)	More Than 10,000 (84)	None (89)	1% To 25% (69)	More Than 25% (44)
	%	%	%	%	%	%	%
Strong possibility	66	59	68	70	58	70	75
Slight possibility	28	31	26	27	30	28	25
No possibility at all	5	10	3	2	9	3	—
Not sure	1	—	3	—	2	—	—

Employee Willingness to Contribute to Pension Plans

Part of the solution to the projected increases in pension costs may lie with employees themselves. A surprisingly high 68% of those currently covered by pension plans say they would be willing to contribute, or to contribute more than they do now, to a pension plan if it increased the benefits they would receive when they retire. Twenty-four percent say they would not be willing to make such contributions. Thus, in general, it may not be unrealistic to expect workers to begin to contribute more than they do now to their pension plan in exchange for increased benefits. Employee willingness to contribute to their pension plan rises to a high 71% among hourly wage workers who are currently covered by a private pension plan.

Business leaders greatly underestimate their employees' willingness to contribute to pension plans. Only 38% feel that a majority of their employees would be willing to contribute or to contribute more than they do now, while 54% feel a majority of their employees would not be willing.

Table VIII-2

WILLINGNESS TO CONTRIBUTE MORE TO PENSION PLAN
FOR INCREASED BENEFITS
(Asked of employees covered by private pension plans and of business leaders)

Q.: Generally, would you be willing to contribute to, or to contribute more than you do now to, a pension plan if it increased the benefits you receive when you retire, or not?

Q.: Generally, do you think a majority of employees would be willing to contribute to, or to contribute more than they do now to, your company's pension plan if it increased the benefits they receive when they retire, or not?

(Number of respondents)	Pension Plan Participants				Total Business Leaders (210)
		Employment			
	Total (593)	Hourly Wage Worker (267)	Salaried (290)	Self-Employed* (28)	
	%	%	%	%	%
Would be willing	68	71	66	63	38
Would not be willing	24	21	27	30	54
Not sure	8	8	8	7	3
Depends (vol.)	x	x	x	x	5

*Sample too small for reliable analysis.
x = not asked of employees.

Employee Willingness to Accept Smaller Pay Increases

Employees are much less willing to accept smaller pay increases in exchange for a larger pension than to make additional contributions to their plan. Just 39% say they would be willing to take a smaller pay increase while 49% would not. Again, the greatest measure of willingness on this measure is found among hourly wage workers, who would be willing to accept smaller pay increases by a razor-thin margin of 46-45%.

Business leaders are much more attuned to their employees' attitudes toward accepting smaller pay increases than they are about attitudes toward increasing pension plan contributions. By 88-6%, most employers feel that a majority of their employees would not be willing to take small pay increases in order to get a larger pension.

Table VIII-3

WILLINGNESS TO TAKE SMALLER PAY INCREASES FOR LARGER PENSION BENEFITS

(Asked of employees covered by private pension plans and of business leaders)

Q.: Would you be willing to take small pay increases in order to get a larger pension, or not?

Q.: Do you think a majority of employees would be willing to take smaller pay increases in order to get a larger pension, or not?

(Number of respondents)	Pension Plan Participants				Total Business Leaders (212)
	Total (593)	Employment			
		Hourly Wage Worker (267)	Salaried (290)	Self-Employed* (28)	
	%	%	%	%	%
Woud be willing	39	46	36	26	6
Would not be willing	49	45	53	52	88
Not sure	11	10	11	22	1
Depends (vol.)	X	X	X	X	5

*Sample too small for reliable analysis.
x = not asked of employees.

Benefits Desired in Exchange for Employee Contributions

More than anything, employees would be willing to increase their contributions to their pension plan if the plan provided benefits that increased with inflation and the cost of living (74-16% willing). By smaller margins, employees say they would be willing to increase contributions if their plan let them become eligible to receive benefits at an earlier age (61-27%), if the plan had a 100% guarantee that they would receive pension benefits (60-29%), and if the plan provided survivor benefits to their spouse (58-31%).

Business leaders underestimate their employees' willingness to contribute more to their pension plan on each of these potential plan provisions. The leaders are most closely attuned to the attitudes of their employees on the question of cost-of-living increases. Fifty percent of the leaders feel a majority of their employees would be willing to contribute to their plan in exchange for benefits that increase with the cost of living, while 32% feel a majority would not be willing to increase contributions for this provision. Only relatively small percentages of the leaders feel that employees would be willing to increase their contributions in exchange for any of the other provisions listed.

Table VIII-4

WILLINGNESS TO CONTRIBUTE MORE TO PENSION PLAN
IF PENSION PROVIDED VARIOUS FEATURES
(Asked of employees covered by private pension plan and of business leaders)

Q.: And would you be willing to contribute to, or to contribute more than you do now, to your pension plan if your pension (ITEM), or not?

Q.: And would a majority of employees be willing to contribute to, or to contribute more than they do now to, their pension plan if their pension (ITEM), or not?

(Number of respondents)		Pension Plan Participants (576)			Business Leaders (208)			
		Willing	Not Willing	Not Sure	Willing	Not Willing	Already Provided (vol.)	Not Sure
Provided benefits that increased with inflation and the cost of living	%	74	16	10	50	32	5	13
Let them become eligible to receive benefits at an earlier age	%	61	27	11	28	36	31	5
Had a 100% guarantee that they would receive pension benefits	%	60	29	11	13	57	25	5
Provided survivor benefits to their spouse	%	58	31	11	18	30	48	4

Benefits Desired in Exchange for Smaller Pension Benefits

In addition to increasing their pension contributions in exchange for various changes in the benefits they will receive, employees say they would be willing to accept smaller pension benefits if their plan provided features such as benefits that increased with the cost of living, earlier benefit eligibility, survivor benefits, and a 100% guarantee of receiving benefits. In general, however, employees are more positively inclined to increase their own contributions in exchange for these provisions.

Again, employees say they are most willing to accept smaller benefits if their pension provided benefits that would increase with inflation and the cost of living. This notion is favored by current pension plan participants by 74-16%. Majorities also say they would be willing to receive smaller benefits if their plan let them become eligible to receive benefits at an earlier age (58-31% willing), and if their plan provided survivor benefits to their spouse (57-32%). Lastly, receiving smaller benefits in exchange for having a 100% guarantee of receiving benefits is favored by a narrow 45-39% plurality.

More than half of the business leaders (58%) are aware of their employees' willingness to receive smaller pension benefits in return for receiving benefits that increase with inflation and the cost of living. They are less positive, as are employees themselves, about employee willingness to accept smaller pension benefits in exchange for the other provisions listed. Also, early retirement benefits, survivor benefits, and guaranteed benefits are already provided by many of the firms interviewed.

Observation:

Certainly these findings should be approached with some caution. The difference between what people say they are willing to accept and what they are actually willing to accept can be considerable, particularly when it concerns their present and future income. However, if employees understand exactly how they will benefit in retired life, they are very likely to make sacrifices today. Increased emphasis on employee contributions to pension plans may provide a way to ease the upward pressure on employers' pension costs while meeting the growing demands of retired workers.

Table VIII-5

WILLINGNESS TO RECEIVE SMALLER PENSION BENEFITS IF PENSION PROVIDED VARIOUS FEATURES

(Asked of employees covered by private pension plans and of business leaders)

Q.: Would you be willing to receive smaller pension benefits in the future if your pension (ITEM), or not?

Q.: Do you think a majority of employees would be willing to receive smaller pension benefits in the future if their pension (ITEM), or not?

(Number of respondents)		Pension Plan Participants (593)			Business Leaders (212)			
		Willing	Not Willing	Not Sure	Willing	Not Willing	Already Provided (vol.)	Not Sure
Provided benefits that increased with inflation and the cost of living	%	74	16	10	58	25	6	11
Let them become eligible to receive benefits at an earlier age	%	58	31	11	35	29	33	4
Provided survivor benefits to their spouse	%	57	32	11	26	19	53	2
Had a 100% guarantee that they would receive pension benefits	%	45	39	15	9	64	25	4

Business Leaders' Attitudes on Employee Contributions

It is interesting to note that while a majority of employees say they would be willing to contribute to their pension plan, most employers do not think they should be required to do so. Just 26% of the leaders interviewed say employees should be required to contribute to their pension plan, and 72% say they should not. Interestingly, nearly 3 of every 4 executives do not feel employees should be required to contribute to their plan.

Though a majority of leaders do not feel employees should be required to contribute, many would be willing to accept a plan with voluntary employee contributions. A total of 61% would prefer some type of employee contribution: 22% would prefer a pension plan that required employee contributions; 39% would prefer a plan with voluntary employee contributions. Still, nearly 4 out of 10 (39%) would prefer a pension plan with no provision for employee contributions.

A desire for employee contributions is strongest among those from companies with 2,000 employees or less and those from companies with more than 10,000 employees.

Table VIII-6

EMPLOYER ATTITUDES TOWARD REQUIRING EMPLOYEE CONTRIBUTIONS TO PENSION PLANS
(Asked of business leaders)

Q.: Do you feel that your employees should be required to make a contribution to the plan, or not?

(Number of respondents)	Total (209)
	%
Should be required	26
Should not	72
Not sure	1

Table VIII-7

EMPLOYER PREFERENCES FOR EMPLOYEE CONTRIBUTIONS TO PENSION PLANS
(Asked of business leaders)

Q.: Generally, which would you prefer for your company — a pension plan that required employee contributions, a plan that called for voluntary employee contributions, or a plan with no provision for employee contributions?

		Number Of Employees		
(Number of respondents)	Total (211)	2,000 Or Less (63)	2,001 To 10,000 (64)	More Than 10,000 (84)
	%	%	%	%
A pension plan that required employee contributions	22	21	27	19
A pension plan with voluntary employee contributions	39	44	28	44
A plan with no employee contributions	39	35	45	37
Not sure	—	—	—	—

Desirable Size of Contributions to Pension Plans

What percentage of their salary would employees be willing to contribute to their pension plans? Nearly 1 out of 3 (31%) are unsure, but of the remainder, 25% say they would be willing to contribute between 9% and 10%, 26% say they would be willing to contribute between 1% and 8%, and 12% say they would be willing to contribute more than 10% of their salary to their pension plan. The mean percentage that employees would be willing to contribute is 8.8%.

As has been shown by previous data, most business leaders feel that employees should not be required to contribute to this plan. Among those who feel employees should contribute, however, the mean percentage that employers feel employees should contribute is 4%.

Table VIII-8

PERCENTAGE OF SALARY WILLING TO CONTRIBUTE TO PENSION PLAN
(Asked of employees covered by private pension plans)

Q.: How much would you be willing to contribute to your pension plan, in terms of a percentage of your salary, so that you would have an adequate retirement income?

(Number of respondents)	Total (582) %
0%	5
1-2%	3
3-4%	2
5-6%	18
7-8%	3
9-10%	25
11-15%	5
16-20%	3
21-30%	3
31% and over	1
Not sure	31
Mean percentage	8.8

Table VIII-9

EMPLOYERS' ATTITUDE TOWARD PERCENTAGE OF SALARY
EMPLOYEES SHOULD CONTRIBUTE TO PENSION PLAN
(Asked of business leaders)

Q.: What percentage of their salary do you think employees should contribute to the plan?

(Number of respondents)	Total (209) %
0%	72
1-2%	5
3-4%	8
5-6%	7
7-8%	2
9-10%	—
11-15%	*
16-20%	*
21-30%	*
31% and over	—
Not sure	1
Mean percentage**	4.0

*Less than 0.5%.
**Mean is computed without "0%" response.

85

Lastly, many employees (33%) do not know what percentage of their salary their employer should contribute to their plan. Among those able to offer an opinion, however, the mean response is a high 14.3%. This is a full 3% higher than employers say they are now paying.

Table VIII-10

PERCENTAGE OF SALARY EMPLOYER SHOULD CONTRIBUTE TO PENSION PLAN
(Asked of employees covered by private pension plans)

Q.: And how much do you think your employer should contribute to your pension plan, as a percentage of your salary, so that you would have an adequate retirement income?

(Number of respondents)	Total (581) %
0%	1
1-2%	3
3-4%	2
5-6%	13
7-8%	3
9-10%	19
11-15%	6
16-20%	4
21-30%	1
31% and over	13
Not sure	33
Mean percentage	14.3

CHAPTER IX:

BUSINESS LEADERS' ATTITUDES
TOWARD PENSIONS AND ERISA

Advantages and Disadvantages of Pension Plans to Companies

Business leaders are firmly committed to private pensions, seeing in them a number of important advantages for their companies. But at the same time, they are deeply concerned about growing pension costs and about the administrative complexity that they believe stems from increased government regulation.

More than anything else, business leaders feel that pensions are a powerful vehicle for attracting and retaining top quality employees. The chief advantage of a pension plan, according to the executives interviewed, is that it permits their company to compete with other companies for the best employees (54%). More than half (52%) feel that it provides a powerful incentive for employees to stay with the firm. Many employers cite the advantages of pensions to employees themselves. One out of three say the main advantage of a pension plan to their company is that it provides security and an orderly future for employees. In addition, 24% feel that it provides an important sense of security for both employees and employers.

But the plans are not without their disadvantages. A high 61% of the leaders cite increasing costs in an inflationary economy as the main disadvantage of a pension plan to their company. One in four feels the main disadvantage is the complexity of administration and paperwork. Similarly, according to 22%, the primary drawbacks of pension plans are the controls and restrictions placed upon them by government.

Table IX-1

ADVANTAGES OF PENSION PLAN TO COMPANIES
(Asked of business leaders)

Q.: Overall, what would you say are the main advantages to your company of a pension plan?

(Number of respondents)	Total (212) %
Can compete with other companies for best employees, bargaining tool	54
Retention of employees, incentive to stay with firm	52
Good/orderly future security benefit plan for employee	33
Sense of security for employee and employer	24
Satisfies company's moral/social responsibility to employee	15
Key/major/standard part of wage/compensation package/plan	10
Incentive to work/be productive	9
Better employee-management relations/morale	9
Money put in can grow, allow employee to build capital for future	8
Incentive to participate in growth and profitability of company	3
Tax benefits, earnings are tax free	3
All other reasons	3
None	*
Not sure	—

*Less than 0.5%.

Table IX-2

DISADVANTAGES OF PENSION PLAN TO COMPANIES
(Asked of business leaders)

Q.: And what would you say are the main disadvantages?

(Number of respondents)	Total (210) %
Increasing costs in an inflationary economy	61
Complexity of administration/paperwork	25
Government controls/restrictions (ERISA)	22
Startling costs but well spent, worth it	2
Mismanagement, increases in Social Security has effect on pension plans	*
All other reasons	13
None	14
Not sure	1

*Less than 0.5%.

Pension Plan Terminations

One of the chief criticisms of the Employee Retirement Income Security Act of 1974 (ERISA) is that the law has significantly increased pension costs and created time-consuming administrative burdens that have resulted in the termination of thousands of plans. According to one source, at least 24,000 programs have been terminated since 1975. Proponents of ERISA argue that the law has had a favorable impact in this regard as it has resulted in terminations primarily among plans that were financially unsound to begin with. Critics argue that the law has done more to reduce the number of people covered by a plan than to prompt pension plan growth, as was originally intended.

Regardless of the merits of either argument, the results here show that the wave of terminations following ERISA has slowed to a trickle. It appears that most plans that were likely candidates for termination have been either already dropped or satisfactorily altered to comply with government regulations.

When asked whether their company has ever considered terminating its employee pension plan in the past ten years, just 5% acknowledge that it has, while 94% claim that they have not considered terminating their plan in the ten-year period. Pension plan terminations are most likely to have been considered by smaller firms. Thirteen percent of those with 2,000 or fewer employees say they have considered terminating their plan, while only 5% offer the same response among companies with between 2,000 and 10,000 employees, and none has considered termination among companies with more than 10,000 employees.

Among the 11 employers (5% of those interviewed) that have considered terminating their plan, 7 mention federal regulations or ERISA as the factor prompting their concern and 6 mention high costs. All 11, however, have decided to continue offering their plan to employees.

Table IX-3

TERMINATION OF PENSION PLAN
(Asked of business leaders)

Q.: In the past ten years has your company ever considered terminating its employee pension plan, or not?

(Number of respondents)	Total (212)	Number Of Employees		
		2,000 Or Less (63)	2,001 To 10,000 (65)	More Than 10,000 (84)
	%	%	%	%
Considered terminating	5	13	5	—
No, not considered	94	86	94	100
Not sure	1	2	2	—

Attitudes on ERISA

Overall, business leaders have a generally negative opinion of ERISA. Only 2% say they feel ERISA is an excellent law, 36% feel it is pretty good, 38% rate it only fair, and 23% say ERISA is a poor law. There is little differentiation in opinions toward ERISA among different sized firms. Roughly 6 out of 10 leaders interviewed give ERISA a negative rating regardless of the number of workers employed by their firm.

Table IX-4

ATTITUDES TOWARD ERISA
(Asked of business leaders)

Q.: Let's talk about ERISA for a minute. Generally, do you feel that ERISA is an excellent, pretty good, only fair, or poor law?

(Number of respondents)	Total (212)	Number Of Employees		
		2,000 Or Less (63)	2,001 To 10,000 (65)	More Than 10,000 (84)
	%	%	%	%
Excellent	2	5	2	1
Pretty good	36	30	40	37
Only fair	38	35	38	39
Poor	23	25	20	23
Not sure	1	5	—	—

Though business leaders are generally negative on ERISA, their views are mixed on the law's specific provisions. For instance, by an overwhelming 90-10%, business leaders approve of the vesting requirements mandated by ERISA. They are also strongly positive in their view of ERISA's pension eligibility requirements (78-20% positive), joint and survivor benefits (87-10%), and IRA and Keogh Plan provisions (85-8%).

Somewhat surprisingly, in light of all the controversy they have engendered, ERISA's funding standards (76-16% positive) and fiduciary standards (76-21%) are also highly favorably regarded by business executives. Milder approval is found for plan termination insurance (58-36%) and for ERISA's investment limitations (55-36%). By a narrow 49-41%, business leaders also mildly favor ERISA's rollover portability provisions.

If one considers their strongly positive views toward many of ERISA's provisions, one wonders why the law is so negatively rated in general among business leaders. The answer lies with the law's reporting and disclosure requirements. Primarily because of the amount of time that executives must personally devote to them, ERISA's reporting and disclosure requirements meet a strong (71-28%) disapproval among business leaders. Lastly, the leaders disapprove of the limitations on pension benefits set by ERISA by 63-28%.

Table IX-5

DEGREE OF APPROVAL OF VARIOUS ITEMS MANDATED BY ERISA
(Asked of business leaders)

Q.: Would you say you strongly approve, mildly approve, mildly disapprove, or strongly disapprove of the (ITEM) mandated by ERISA?

(Number of respondents: 212)		Strongly Approve	Mildly Approve	Mildly Disapprove	Strongly Disapprove	Not Sure
Pension eligibility requirements	%	33	45	14	6	1
Vesting requirements	%	43	47	6	4	*
Joint and survivor benefits	%	48	39	6	4	4
Funding standards	%	39	37	15	1	7
Portability provisions[1]	%	17	32	23	18	11
Plan termination insurance	%	22	36	19	17	5
Fiduciary standards	%	34	42	15	6	4
Reporting and disclosure requirements	%	7	21	33	38	1
Limitations on pension requirements	%	4	24	33	30	8
Individual retirement plans, IRA and Keogh	%	52	33	5	3	7
Investment limitations	%	13	42	27	9	9

*Less than 0.5%.
[1] Portability provisions refers to rollover.

Business leaders were asked about the impact of ERISA on their particular company. Again, their reviews are mixed.

According to the leaders interviewed, ERISA has generally had either a positive impact or no impact on 7 of the 9 items listed. However, its effects have been negative on two important concerns: the cost of having a pension plan; and the time executives must spend in dealing with pension matters. By 54-30%, business leaders say ERISA has had a negative impact on the cost to their company of having a pension plan. And by 57-34%, they say the law has negatively affected the time executives must spend dealing with pension matters.

Business leaders are strongly positive about the effect ERISA has had on their employees' knowledge about their pension plan (63-5% positive), and about their employees confidence that they will receive the benefits they have been promised (38-1%). At the same time, 6 in 10 feel that ERISA has had no impact on their employees' confidence in their pension plan. More than 1 in 3 (35%) feel ERISA has had no impact on the way pension plans are funded in general, though others feel its impact has been positive by 46-15%.

Majorities feel that ERISA has had no impact on the level at which their company's pension plan is funded, the investment performance of their pension funds, and the economic security of their company's future retirees.

Lastly, 74% say that ERISA has had no impact on the economic health of their company, while 19% say its impact has been negative. Just 6% feel that ERISA has had a positive effect on their company's economic health.

Table IX-6

IMPACT OF ERISA ON COMPANIES AND EMPLOYEES
(Asked of business leaders)

Q.: What impacts has ERISA had on (ITEM) — a very positive impact, a somewhat positive impact, a somewhat negative impact, a very negative impact, or no impact at all?

(Number of respondents: 211)		Very Positive Impact	Somewhat Positive Impact	Somewhat Negative Impact	Very Negative Impact	No Impact At All	Not Sure
The cost to your company of having a pension plan	%	13	17	42	12	15	2
The time executives in your company spend dealing with pension matters	%	18	16	30	27	9	—
The way pension plans are funded in general	%	8	38	14	1	35	3
The level at which your company's pension plan is funded	%	2	15	6	1	73	3
The investment performance of pension funds	%	2	18	14	3	57	5
The knowledge your employees have about their pension plan	%	8	55	3	2	32	*
Your employees' confidence that they will receive the benefits they have been promised	%	8	30	*	1	60	*
The economic health of your company	%	2	4	19	*	74	*
The economic security of your company's future retirees	%	5	23	2	—	69	1

*Less than 0.5%.

Many have said that ERISA's "prudent man" rule has made pension fund managers overly cautious and generally resulted in lower returns. For the most part, however, this is not a view shared by the nation's business executives.

A full 69% of the leaders interviewed feel that ERISA has had little or no effect on the basic investment strategy for their company's pension fund. Another 14% claim that the funding and fiduciary requirements of ERISA have resulted in different, but not necessarily more conservative, investment strategies for pension funds. Just 15% charge that ERISA's funding and fiduciary requirements have resulted in more conservative investment strategies for their company.

Conservative investment strategies prompted by ERISA are slightly more likely to occur among companies relatively small in pension plan assets. Among the companies whose pension plan assets are between $10 million and $69 million, for instance, 23% say ERISA has led to more conservative investment strategies. But the problem is almost non-existent among larger funds. Only 4% of leaders in companies whose pension plan assets total $250 million or more believe their fund investment strategies are more conservative as a result of ERISA.

Observation:

These findings set the record straight on the business community's reactions to ERISA. They will be of considerable interest to the law's proponents and opponents alike. Many of the major criticisms of the law, such as its effect on investment performance, fiduciary standards, and pension eligibility requirements, are not shared by the bulk of business executives. Business's concern about ERISA focuses sharply on pension costs and the time required to administer a plan. Importantly, it should be understood that the leaders' concern about cost relates only partly to the contribution a company makes to its employees' pension fund. By 76-16%, executives are strongly positive about the funding standards set by ERISA, and a large majority feel that the law has not had any impact on the overall economic health of their company. Instead, much of their concern about the cost stems from the high cost of executive time required to deal with pension matters, particularly the time required to meet ERISA's reporting and disclosure requirements. Notwithstanding the problem of pension costs, many of the business community's concerns about pensions and objections to ERISA may be mitigated by easing the administrative burden and costly paperwork that beset regulated private pension plans.

Table IX-7

EFFECT OF ERISA ON PENSION FUND INVESTMENTS
(Asked of business leaders)

Q.: Which one of the statements on this card best represents the effect that ERISA has had on the investments made with your company's pension funds?

(Number of respondents)	Total (211)	Pension Plan Assets			
		Less Than $10 Million (51)	$10 Million To $69 Million (56)	$70 Million To $249 Million (50)	$250 Million Or More (45)
	%	%	%	%	%
Little or no effect	69	69	63	70	78
More conservative investment strategies	15	18	23	12	4
Different, but not necessarily more conservative strategies	14	10	13	18	18
Not sure	2	4	2	—	—

CHAPTER X:

AN EMPLOYEE AND LEADERSHIP ASSESSMENT
OF SOCIAL SECURITY

Confidence in Social Security

The Social Security System has been the target of increasing criticism in recent years. The adverse publicity has instilled concern and skepticism among current and retired employees about the financial stability of the Social Security System.

More than 3 of every 4 (78%) employees and retirees understand that Social Security taxes are used to pay for benefits that people are collecting today, while 8% believe the taxes people pay are set aside in a fund for their own retirement, and 14% are unsure. This understanding of how Social Security is funded is fairly widespread, regardless of educational attainment.

Table X-1

PERCEIVED USE OF SOCIAL SECURITY TAXES
(Asked of current and retired employees)

Q.: Let's talk about Social Security for a minute. As far as you know, do the Social Security taxes people pay get set aside in a fund for their own retirement, or are they used to pay for Social Security benefits that people are collecting today?

		Education		
(Number of respondents)	Total (1688)	8th Grade (209)	High School (755)	College (723)
	%	%	%	%
Get set aside	8	9	9	7
Are used today	78	63	76	85
Not sure	14	28	15	8

One of the implications of the direct funding of Social Security benefits is that Social Security taxes will have to increase as the number of retirees increases over the next several decades. But current and retired employees are not at all confident in the willingness of future generations to pay higher Social Security taxes. Only 12% have a great deal of confidence that future generations will be willing to pay higher Social Security taxes, while 41% have some confidence, and another 41% have hardly any confidence at all.

Significantly, confidence on this question is lowest among those who are most likely to be paying increased Social Security taxes. Forty-six percent of those between 18 and 24 years old and a full 50% of those between 25 and 34 years old have hardly any confidence in the willingness of future generations to pay higher Social Security taxes.

Business leaders share the skepticism of younger employees. An even half of the leaders interviewed have hardly any confidence in the willingness of future generations to pay higher taxes for Social Security, and 44% have some confidence. Only 6% voice a great deal of confidence on this question.

Table X-2

CONFIDENCE IN FUTURE GENERATIONS
TO PAY HIGHER SOCIAL SECURITY TAXES
(Asked of current and retired employees)

Q.: Actually, Social Security taxes are used to pay for benefits that people are receiving today. What this means is that if people are going to receive Social Security benefits in the future, the money is going to have to come from taxes paid by future generations. Since the number of older people in this country is going to increase continuously over the next several decades, the tax burden on future generations will also increase. How much confidence do you have in the willingness of future generations to pay higher taxes for Social Security benefits for retirees — a great deal of confidence, some confidence, or hardly any confidence at all?

(Number of respondents)	Total (1686)	Age 18-24 (150)	25-34 (377)	35-49 (435)	50-64 (423)	65 And Over (300)
	%	%	%	%	%	%
A great deal of confidence	12	13	10	11	15	13
Some confidence	41	34	38	42	44	45
Hardly any confidence	41	46	50	45	37	30
Not sure	5	6	2	2	5	12

Table X-3

BUSINESS LEADER CONFIDENCE IN WILLINGNESS OF
FUTURE GENERATIONS TO PAY HIGHER SOCIAL SECURITY TAXES
(Asked of business leaders)

Q.: How much confidence do you have in the willingness of future generations to pay higher taxes for Social Security benefits for retirees — a great deal of confidence, some confidence, or hardly any confidence at all?

(Number of respondents)	Total (212)
	%
Great deal of confidence	6
Some confidence	44
Hardly any confidence	50
Not sure	*

*Less than 0.5%.

Of equal concern is people's confidence in the ability of the Social Security System to pay them benefits when they retire. More than 2 out of 5 (42%) have hardly any confidence that the present Social Security System will be able to pay them benefits when they retire. In total, 55% have at least some confidence, 40% have some confidence, and 15% have a great deal of confidence.

Again, confidence in Social Security is particularly low among younger age groupings. Roughly half of those between 18 and 34 years of age have hardly any confidence in Social Security's ability to pay them benefits, and 43% express the same view in the 35 to 49 age group. Confidence in Social Security is highest among those 50 years or older.

The business community is somewhat more confident about Social Security's ability to pay benefits to future retirees. One in four have hardly any confidence in Social Security's ability to pay, 54% have some confidence, and 19% express a great deal of confidence.

Observation:

These findings provide another early warning signal of trouble ahead. An overwhelming majority of today's work force is counting on Social Security to provide income when they retire. Yet substantial numbers, particularly among younger employees, have little confidence in Social Security's ability to pay their retirement benefits. And one does not have to depend solely on the findings presented here to know that the public is becoming increasingly opposed — and actively resistant — to higher taxes. Increasing skepticism about the Social Security System, along with a growing demand for retirement income, is likely to bring a substantial upsurge of political pressure on government and the Social Security System. Raising Social Security taxes, an approach used more or less successfully in the past, is less and less likely to receive an enthusiastic response. Alternative funding policies and other sources of retirement income are likely to be turned to as alternatives to increasing Social Security taxes.

Table X-4

CONFIDENCE IN SOCIAL SECURITY TO PAY RETIREMENT BENEFITS
(Asked of current employees)

Q.: And how much confidence do you have that the present Social Security System will be able to pay you benefits when you retire — a great deal, some, or hardly any confidence at all?

		Age				
		18- 24	25- 34	35- 49	50- 64	65 And Over
(Number of respondents)	Total (1682)	(148)	(380)	(434)	(422)	(297)
	%	%	%	%	%	%
A great deal	15	12	9	9	28	34
Some	40	35	35	44	42	38
Hardly any	42	50	52	43	28	10
Not applicable	1	—	2	1	1	10
Not sure	2	3	2	2	2	7

Table X-5

BUSINESS LEADER CONFIDENCE IN SOCIAL SECURITY SYSTEM
(Asked of business leaders)

Q.: And how much confidence do you have that the present Social Security System will be able to pay benefits to your employees when they retire — a great deal, some, or hardly any confidence at all?

(Number of respondents)	Total (209)
	%
A great deal	19
Some	54
Hardly any	25
Not applicable (vol.)	1
Not sure	1

The Role of Social Security During Retirement

An overwhelming majority of current and retired employees understand that Social Security is intended to provide a basic level of retirement income, to be supplemented with other sources of income. Most are well aware that Social Security alone will not provide enough to live on. By 77-19%, current and retired employees reject the statement, "I don't have to worry about my retirement, because Social Security will take care of me." Moreover, the bulk of the survey respondents believe that providing a basic level of retirement income is the role that Social Security should have in our society.

If one considers their relatively low assessment of Social Security compared with public and private pension plans, and their lack of confidence in Social Security's ability to pay benefits to future retirees, it comes as no surprise that current and retired employees have little enthusiasm for the notion of providing all retirement income through Social Security. By 76-17%, current and retired employees feel that Social Security's proper role should be to provide a basic level of retirement income, and not all retirement income.

Thirty-one percent of those interviewed feel Social Security should provide a basic level of retirement income, taking into account a person's previous income. More than 1 in 5 (22%) feel Social Security should provide a basic level of retirement income, regardless of a person's pre-retirement income. Another 23% feel Social Security should be used to provide a basic level of income which should provide a supplement to other retirement income.

Lower income groups are most likely to feel that all retirement income should be provided through Social Security, although the notion is supported by no more than 1 in 5 among those earning under $15,000 a year. Generally speaking, there is little variation in the public's attitudes toward the proper role of Social Security, regardless of income group.

Respondents who indicated they felt that Social Security should provide all retirement income were asked whether they would still favor the idea if it meant a possible increase in taxes. Those favoring an increased role for Social Security split down the middle on this question, with 39% opposing an increased role for Social Security if it meant an increase in taxes, and 38% favoring it regardless of the tax consequences (23% were not sure).

Table X-6

ATTITUDES TOWARD THE PREFERRED ROLE OF SOCIAL SECURITY
(Asked of current and retired employees)

Q.: People have different ideas about what the role of Social Security should be in our society. Which one of the statements on this card best describes the role you feel Social Security should have?

(Number of respondents)	Total (1681)	Income			
		Under $7M (232)	$7M-14,999 (532)	$15M-24,999 (551)	$25M And Over (309)
	%	%	%	%	%
Provide a basic level of retirement income, regardless of a person's pre-retirement income	22	28	20	24	19
Provide a basic level of retirement income, taking into account a person's previous income	31	26	32	33	29
Provide a basic level of retirement income, to be used as a supplement to other retirement income	23	10	19	24	37
Provide all retirement income, either regardless of a person's pre-retirement income, or by taking a person's previous income into account	11	12	12	9	8
Provide all retirement income, taking a person's previous income into account up to a certain cut-off point	6	8	7	7	4
Not sure	7	16	9	4	4

Table X-7

SUPPORT FOR PROVIDING ALL RETIREMENT INCOME THROUGH
SOCIAL SECURITY WITH AN INCREASE IN TAXES
(Asked of those who feel Social Security
should provide all retirement income)

Q.: Suppose providing all retirement income through Social Security meant a sizeable increase in taxes. Would you still favor providing all retirement income through Social Security, or not?

(Number of respondents)	Total (385)
	%
Favor	38
Oppose	39
Not sure	23

Virtually every business leader interviewed believes that Social Security should provide a basic level of retirement income. Forty-five percent believe it should be used as a supplement to other retirement income. Thirty-two percent believe that Social Security should provide a basic level of income while taking into account a person's previous income, and 21% believe it should provide a basic level regardless of a person's pre-retirement income.

97

Table X-8

BUSINESS LEADER ATTITUDES TOWARD THE
PREFERRED ROLE OF SOCIAL SECURITY
(Asked of business leaders)

Q.: People have different ideas about what the role of Social Security should be in our society. Which one of the statements on this card best describes the role you feel Social Security should have?

(Number of respondents)	Total (212)
	%
Provide a basic level of retirement income, regardless of a person's pre-retirement income	21
Provide a basic level of retirement income, taking into account a person's previous income	32
Provide a basic level of retirement income, to be used as a supplement to other retirement income	45
Provide all retirement income, either regardless of a person's pre-retirement income, or by taking a person's previous income into account	*
Provide all retirement income, taking a person's previous income into account up to a certain cut-off point	*
Not sure	1

*Less than 0.5%.

Part of the reason for low interest among current and retired employees in having all retirement income provided through Social Security is a lack of confidence in the government's ability to manage such a program. Nearly half the respondents (49%) have hardly any confidence in the government's ability to run a program in which all retirement income would be distributed through the federal government and funded by taxes. Another 37% have some confidence in the government's ability to handle such a plan, while only 10% have a great deal of confidence.

Business leaders have even less confidence in the government's ability to manage such a plan, with 85% giving the "no confidence" response.

Table X-9

CONFIDENCE IN GOVERNMENT'S ABILITY TO MANAGE PLAN TO FUND ALL RETIREMENT INCOME THROUGH TAXES
(Asked of current and retired employees and of business leaders)

Q.: Suppose all retirement income in this country were funded by taxes and distributed through the federal government. How much confidence do you have in the government's ability to manage such a plan — a great deal of confidence, some confidence, or hardly any confidence at all?

(Number of respondents)	Total Current And Retired Employees (1682)	Total Business Leaders (212)
	%	%
Great deal	10	2
Some	37	13
Hardly any at all	49	85
Not sure	4	*

*Less than 0.5%.

Alternative Revenue Sources for Social Security

The future is likely to bring a sharp increase in demands for larger Social Security benefits. A sizeable 80% of current and retired employees feel that Social Security benefits should be increased with the cost of living over the next five years, as is now in effect. Another 6% feel benefits should be increased faster than the cost of living. Less than 1 in 10 (9%) feel Social Security benefits should be kept the same over the next five years, and virtually no one supports the prospect of reducing benefits.

A sizeable majority (62%) of business leaders share employee attitudes toward increasing Social Security benefits with the cost of living. However, a substantial 1 in 3 feel that Social Security benefits should be kept the same.

Table X-10

WHAT SHOULD HAPPEN TO SOCIAL SECURITY BENEFITS OVER THE NEXT 5 YEARS
(Asked of current and retired employees and of business leaders)

Q.: And generally, over the next 5 years, do you think Social Security benefits should be reduced, kept the same, increased with the cost of living, or increased faster than the cost of living?

(Number of respondents)	Total Current And Retired Employees (1692)	Total Business Leaders (212)
	%	%
Be reduced	2	4
Kept the same	9	33
Increased with the cost of living	80	62
Increased faster than the cost of living	6	*
Not sure	2	1

*Less than 0.5%.

A previously discussed finding shows that a majority of current and retired employees agree in principle that more money should be collected from working people so that the income of retirees can keep up with inflation. The results here show that people have mixed views as to what moneys should be used to provide benefits to current retirees.

When asked about the recent legislation raising the Social Security tax, a full 77% of current and retired employees agree that additional funds should have been found for Social Security, and only 7% feel that Social Security taxes should have been kept the same with a reduction in Social Security benefits. However, by 47-30%, the sample would have preferred that other taxes be used to help support Social Security, rather than increasing Social Security taxes.

Nearly half (49%) of the business leaders interviewed agree that Social Security taxes should have been increased, while 23% feel that other taxes should have been used to help support Social Security. More than 1 in 5 (22%) feel that Social Security taxes should have been kept the same with a reduction in the benefits paid out.

Table X-11

ATTITUDES TOWARD RECENT SOCIAL SECURITY TAX HIKE
(Asked of current and retired employees and of business leaders)

Q.: (As you know,) last year Congress passed a law that increases the Social Security taxes paid by employers and employees every year for the next 10 years. This was done so that the funds coming into the Social Security System could keep up with the benefits being paid out. Before the law was passed, more money was being paid out than was being collected. Which do you think should have been done — to increase Social Security taxes, to keep Social Security taxes the same and reduce the benefits being paid out, or to keep Social Security taxes the same and use other taxes to help support Social Security?

(Number of respondents)	Total Current And Retired Employees (1675)	Total Business Leaders (209)
	%	%
Increase Social Security taxes	30	49
Reduce benefits	7	22
Use other taxes	47	23
Not sure	16	5

Current and retired employees split down the middle on the question of what tax moneys should be used to support Social Security. Forty-five percent feel Social Security benefits should be paid from Social Security taxes, and a marginally smaller 42% feel that part of the money should come from other taxes. Just 5% feel that all Social Security benefits should be paid from other taxes, but this results in a total of 47% who feel that all or part of the money required for Social Security benefits should come from sources other than Social Security taxes.

Business leaders have a sharply divergent view. Only 1 in 5 feels that all or part of Social Security moneys should come from other taxes: 17% feel part of the money should come from other taxes, while 3% feel it should all come from other taxes. A 79% majority think Social Security benefits should be paid entirely from Social Security taxes.

Observation:

Again, the findings suggest increased political pressure on Social Security in the future, much of which may be in the form of an increased demand to use general revenues or other revenue sources to fund Social Security. Employees are strongly behind the notion of providing benefits that increase with the cost of living and inflation, and the demands upon the Social Security system are likely to be considerable. At the same time, raising Social Security taxes further is likely to meet with stiff opposition. As demands for increased benefits rise, law-makers and the public are likely to look more favorably upon general revenues as a source for Social Security funds.

Table X-12

PREFERRED MEANS OF FUNDING SOCIAL SECURITY
(Asked of current and retired employees and of business leaders)

Q.: In general, do you think Social Security benefits should be paid from Social Security taxes, or should all or part of the money come from other sources?

(Number of respondents)	Total Current And Retired Employees (1684)	Total Business Leaders (212)
	%	%
Social Security taxes	45	79
All from other taxes	5	3
Part from other taxes	42	17
Not sure	9	1

Opting Out of Social Security

Currently, people who work for federal, state or local governments do not have to be covered by Social Security, while people who work for private companies must be covered and pay Social Security taxes. Few people among the public or the business community are satisfied with this situation.

Only 12% of current and retired employees feel that the present system covering only private sector employees should remain as it is. Nearly half (49%) feel that all workers should be part of the Social Security System, while a smaller but substantial 34% feel that workers themselves or a company should be able to decide if they want to become a part of the Social Security System.

Employees covered by a private pension plan are most likely to feel that all workers should be part of Social Security (52%). However, the same response is found among a 40% plurality of those covered by public pension plans. Only 19% of those covered by public plans feel the present system should remain as it is.

Business leaders voice a strong consensus (68%) for including all workers in the Social Security System. Another 20% of the leaders feel that people themselves or companies should be able to decide about involvement in Social Security, and only 9% feel the present system should remain.

Table X-13

WHETHER ALL WORKERS SHOULD PARTICIPATE IN SOCIAL SECURITY SYSTEM
(Asked of current and retired employees and of business leaders)

Q.: Currently, people who work for federal, state or local governments don't have to be covered by or pay taxes to the Social Security System if their employees choose not to be covered. Do you think that all workers should be required to be part of the Social Security System, that people who work for themselves or a company should be able to decide if they want to be part of the Social Security System, or should the present system remain as it is? (Asked of business leaders)

Q.: Right now people who work for themselves or for a company are covered by Social Security and must pay Social Security taxes. However, people who work for federal, state or local governments are not always covered by or required to pay taxes to the Social Security System if they choose not to. Do you think that all workers should be required to be part of the Social Security System, that people who work for themselves or a company should be able to decide if they want to be part of the Social Security System, or should the present system remain as it is? (Asked of current and retired employees)

| (Number of respondents) | Total Current and Retired Employees (1685) | Current Employees | | | | Total Business Leaders (212) |
		Total (1320)	Covered By Private Plan (688)	Covered By Public Plan (229)	Not Covered (456)	
	%	%	%	%	%	%
All workers should be part	49	48	52	40	47	68
People should be able to decide	34	37	35	37	38	20
Present system should remain	12	11	11	19	9	9
Not sure	5	4	3	4	6	2

Permitting individuals or companies to leave the Social Security System at will would clearly lead to a significant decrease in the number of people covered by Social Security. If they could choose whether or not to be covered by Social Security, 26% of current and retired employees and 32% of those currently employed would choose to leave the system, while 68% and 61%, respectively, would stay in.

The figures are even more striking among business executives. Thirty-seven percent of the executives interviewed would pull their company out of the Social Security System if they had the choice, while 61% would choose to remain in the system. And more than half (52%) of those in firms with between 2,001 and 10,000 employees would opt out of Social Security if they could.

Table X-14

WHETHER WOULD CHOOSE TO PARTICIPATE IN SOCIAL SECURITY SYSTEM
(Asked of current and retired employees and of business leaders)

Q.: If you could choose whether or not you/your company would be in the Social Security System, what would you choose — to be in the Social Security System or to get out of the system?

(Number of respondents)	Total Current And Retired Em- ployees (1687)	Current Employees				Total Retired Em- ployees (393)	Business Leaders			
		Total (1322)	Covered By Private Plan (692)	Covered By Public Plan (229)	Not Covered (455)		Total (211)	Number Of Employees		
								2,000 Or Less (63)	2,001 To 10,000 (65)	More Than 10,000 (83)
	%	%	%	%	%	%	%	%	%	%
To be in Social Security	68	61	60	55	66	88	61	63	46	70
To get out	26	32	33	37	29	7	37	35	52	27
Not sure	7	7	8	8	6	5	2	2	2	4

CHAPTER XI:

PUBLIC PENSIONS: SOME POLICY CONSIDERATIONS

Attitudes Toward Regulation of Public Plans

Strong majorities of current and retired employees and of business leaders feel that public pension plans should be subject to the same regulations for funding, reporting, and eligibility requirements as are private pensions. Public plan compliance with private plan regulations is favored by 68% of current and retired employees (14% opposed), and by an overwhelming 93% of business leaders. Moreover, such compliance is favored by a sizeable 65% majority of employees currently covered by public plans and opposed by only 18%.

For the most part, current and retired employees feel that public and private pensions should be subject to the same regulations because they believe all workers should be treated equally. Respondents seem to feel that the current system affords public employees special advantages, and they favor public and private plan compliance because it will eliminate these advantages. Those opposed to bringing public plans under private pension regulations say that the government is different because it is larger than private companies and that public plans cannot be run in the same manner as private plans.

Business leaders also feel that it would be fairer if public pensions fell under the same regulations as private pensions. They are also concerned that the benefits in public plans are established with no concern for funding adequacy, and that private pension disclosure regulations should be followed because the public has a right to know how government plans are managed. Also, many feel there should be more fiduciary responsibility in government. Interestingly, relatively few people among business leaders or current and retired employees mention the problem of double dipping as a reason for public plan compliance with private plan regulations.

Table XI-1

WHETHER PUBLIC PENSIONS SHOULD BE SUBJECT TO SAME REGULATIONS AS PRIVATE PENSIONS
(Asked of current and retired employees and of business leaders)

Q.: (As you know,) right now, pension funds for government employees are not subject to the same controls or regulations as private pension funds such as funding, reporting and eligibility requirements. Do you think these public pensions should be subject to the same regulations as private pensions, or not?

(Number of respondents)	Current And Retired Employees (1688)	Current Employees				Total Business Leaders (212)
		Total (1322)	Covered By Private Plan (692)	Covered By Public Plan (230)	Not Covered (454)	
	%	%	%	%	%	%
Should be subject to same regulation	68	72	75	65	70	93
Should not be subject to same regulation	14	14	14	18	14	6
Not sure	18	14	11	16	17	1

Table XI-2

WHY PUBLIC PENSIONS SHOULD OR SHOULD NOT BE SUBJECT TO SAME REGULATIONS AS PRIVATE ONES
(Asked of current and retired employees)

Q.: Why do you say that? Anything else?

(Number of respondents: 1579)	Total Current And Retired Employees %
It should be more fair, all workers should be treated equally	25
Should be same regulations/controls for all	19
There should be no difference, all pension plans should be same	15
Government employees should get no special treatment/advantages	14
Public has a right to know what government is doing; accountability	7
We pay taxes, government workers get benefits, loopholes	7
Government employees are no better than anyone else	6
Danger of abuse/corruption/double dipping by government employees	5
Government is different/larger, cannot be run same	4
Government is more stable, assured future	4
Private company should have individually based pensions	3
There are too many government controls on everything already	1
Government should stay out of business/free enterprise	1
Any other answer	8
Not sure	16

Table XI-3

BUSINESS LEADERS' ATTITUDES TOWARD WHY PUBLIC PENSIONS SHOULD OR SHOULD NOT BE SUBJECT TO SAME REGULATIONS AS PRIVATE ONES
(Asked of business leaders)

Q.: Why do you say that? Anything else?

(Number of respondents)	Total (208) %
Should be same regulations/controls for all	35
Government employees should get no special advantages	16
Benefits established with no concern for ability to fund	15
Public has right to know, accountability	14
There should be no difference	13
It should be more fair	13
Should be more fiduciary responsibility to government	13
Government employees are no better than others	10
We pay the taxes, government workers get the benefits	10
Danger of abuse/corruption/double dipping	7
Should make some people get benefits they have been promised	5
Private companies should not have to compete with excessive government benefits	5
Government is more stable, more assured future	3
Too many government controls on everything already	2
Just creates more paperwork and red tape/adds to bureaucracy	2
Government is different/larger, cannot be run the same	1
Same level of funding adequacy impractical considering fiscal and tax implications	1
Government should stay out of business	*
Private company should have individually based pensions	—
All other	—
Not sure	*

*Less than 0.5%.

Survey respondents were also asked specifically whether the eligibility requirements for government pensions should be the same as those for private pensions and whether public pensions should be funded on the same basis as private pension plans. In both instances, majorities of business leaders and of current and retired employees favor public plan compliance with private regulations.

By 65-19%, current and retired employees think the eligibility for government pensions should be the same as that for private pensions. This proposal is also favored by employees covered by public pension plans, though the margin here is a narrower 50-36%. Public plan compliance with private plan eligibility requirements is favored by an overwhelming 98% of all business leaders interviewed.

Including the funding of government pension plans on the same basis as company plans is favored by a two-thirds majority of current and retired employees. Support for the idea is consistently strong, whether an employee is covered by a private plan or a public plan. Also, the funding measure draws a 90% favorable response from business leaders.

Table XI-4

ATTITUDES TOWARD PUBLIC PLAN COMPLIANCE WITH
PRIVATE PLAN ELIGIBILITY REQUIREMENTS
(Asked of current and retired employees and of business leaders)

Q.: (And now this one) Under most private pension plans, full pension benefits are not generally payable until a person reaches 65 years of age. These benefits are paid out of funds that have been invested in previous years. Under some government pensions plans, full pensions are generally payable after 29 years of service, regardless of a person's age. These benefits are generally paid for out of current taxes. Would you favor or oppose making the eligibility requirements for government pensions the same as the eligibility requirements for private pensions?

(Number of respondents)	Total Current And Retired Employees (1686)	Current Employees				Total Business Leaders (212)
		Total (1323)	Covered By Private Plan (692)	Covered By Public Plan (230)	Not Covered (455)	
	%	%	%	%	%	%
Favor	65	68	72	50	67	98
Oppose	19	20	19	36	16	*
Not sure	16	13	10	14	17	1

*Less than 0.5%.

Table XI-5

ATTITUDES TOWARD PUBLIC PLAN COMPLIANCE WITH
PRIVATE PLAN FUNDING REQUIREMENTS
(Asked of current and retired employees and of business leaders)

Q.: Presently, companies with pension plans are required to set aside money today for the future pension benefits of their current employees. Most government plans do not fund pensions this way, but use today's taxes for today's pension benefits. This means lower taxes today, but probably higher taxes or lower benefits for government workers tomorrow. Would you favor or oppose putting the funding of government pension plans on the same basis as company pension plans?

Q.: Presently, ERISA requires companies with pension plans to set aside money today for the future pension benefits of their current employees. As you know, most government plans do not pre-fund, but use today's taxes for today's pension benefits. Would you favor or oppose putting the funding of government pension plans on the same basis as company pension plans?

(Number of respondents)	Total Current And Retired Employees (1685)	Current Employees				Total Business Leaders (212)
		Total (1320)	Covered By Private Plan (690)	Covered By Public Plan (230)	Not Covered (454)	
	%	%	%	%	%	%
Favor	66	68	70	69	65	90
Oppose	16	16	15	18	15	8
Not sure	18	16	14	12	20	2

Double Dipping

There has been much discussion about double dipping, a term that generally refers to the practice of retiring early from a job to work at another job, then retiring from the second job to collect pensions from both. Critics of this practice have focused primarily on government employees who sometimes may retire from a job after as little as 20 years' service. The results here show that there is only mild public opposition to the practice of double dipping.

By 51-42%, a narrow majority of current and retired employees believe that people who retire after 20 years of service on a government job should be able to collect a government pension while working at a second job. Support for this notion is strongest among employees covered by public pension plans (64-32%), though it is also supported by a majority (51-43%) among those covered by private plans. Business leaders take an opposite view, believing by 50-30% that retired government workers should not be able to collect a government pension while working at a second job.

Respondents were also asked whether people who retire after 20 years of government service and who then work and retire from a second job should be able to collect two pensions — one for each job they have had. Strong support for this measure is found among both business leaders and current and retired employees. Sixty-seven percent of current and retired employees and 82% of business leaders believe that people who work two jobs should be able to collect two pensions.

Table XI-6

ATTITUDE TOWARD RETIRED GOVERNMENT WORKERS COLLECTING A PENSION WHILE WORKING A SECOND JOB
(Asked of current and retired employees and of business leaders)

Q.: Suppose people who retire after 20 years of service on a government job begin working at another job. Should these people be able to collect a government pension while they are working at a second job, or not?

(Number of respondents)	Total Current And Retired Employees (1687)	Current Employees				Total Business Leaders (212)
		Total (1323)	Covered By Private Plan (693)	Covered By Public Plan (230)	Not Covered (454)	
	%	%	%	%	%	%
Should be able	51	52	51	64	49	30
Should not	42	42	43	32	43	60
Depends (vol.)	—	—	—	—	—	8
Not sure	7	7	6	4	8	1

Table XI-7

ATTITUDE TOWARD RETIRED GOVERNMENT WORKERS
COLLECTING TWO PENSIONS
(Asked of current and retired employees and of business leaders)

Q.: Now suppose people who retired after 20 years of government service work at another job until they reach the normal retirement age for that second job. Should these people be able to collect two pensions — one for each job they have had — or not?

(Number of respondents)	Total Current And Retired Employees (1689)	Current Employees				Total Business Leaders (212)
		Total (1323)	Covered By Private Plan (692)	Covered By Public Plan (230)	Not Covered (455)	
	%	%	%	%	%	%
Should be able	67	69	70	79	65	82
Should not	28	26	26	17	28	14
Not sure	6	5	4	4	7	4

Today, approximately 3% of those who are working full-time have retired from a previous job. Working at a second job after having retired from a first job occurs more frequently among those covered by a public pension plan (5%) than among those covered by a private plan (2%).

Table XI-8

WHETHER RETIRED FROM A PREVIOUS JOB
(Asked of current employees)

Q.: Before you had your present job, did you have another job that you retired from, or not?

(Number of respondents)	Total (1320)	Covered By Private Plan (687)	Covered By Public Plan (227)	Not Covered (440)
	%	%	%	%
Retired from another job	3	2	5	3
Did not retire from another job	97	98	95	98

APPENDIX:

METHODOLOGY

Fieldwork

All the data for this survey were collected from in-person interviews conducted by Harris interviewers, under the control and supervision of the Harris Field Director and Regional Supervisors. Fifteen percent of all interviews were validated by telephone to ensure that the interviews had been honestly and accurately carried out.

All the interviews with the leadership groups were carried out by executive interviewers belonging to the Harris executive field force, under the control of the Executive Field Director, in August 1978.

The Sample Design

A. The national cross-section of current and retired employees: The sample was designed to be representative of the adult civilian population 21 years or older, who are currently or were formerly full-time employees. It is restricted to the continental United States, excluding Alaska and Hawaii, and excluding those in prisons or hospitals. The sample design was based on updated census information on the population of each state, and on the population living in urbanized areas and in more rural areas throughout the country. The sample was stratified to ensure that it would reflect within one percentage point the actual proportion of those living in different regions and in different size of place areas (city, suburb, town, rural). Within each stratum the selection of the ultimate sampling unit (a cluster of adjacent households) was achieved by multi-stage cluster sampling. Within each of sixteen strata (four regions within four size of place categories) first states, then counties, then minor civil divisions and, where possible, census tracts and city blocks were selected proportional to census estimates of their respective populations.

In a proportional sample, the number of interviews that would be obtained with respondents who had retired from full-time work would have been too small for reliable analysis. Therefore, the cross-section contains an oversample of respondents retired from full-time work. The oversample was then statistically reweighted to its proportionate size within the larger sample. Thus, the cross-section is a proportionate representation of current and retired full-time employees.

Interviewers in the field were provided with detailed maps of the ultimate sampling units, and conducted interviews within the assigned respective areas. The national sample consisted of 200 such interviewing areas (sample points) throughout the country. At each sample point one respondent from each of eight different households was interviewed. At each household the respondent was chosen by means of a random selection pattern geared to the number of adults of each sex living in that household. The representativeness of the sample is shown in the following table:

PROFILE OF THE PUBLIC SAMPLE OF CURRENT AND RETIRED EMPLOYEES

	Number in Sample*	Weighted Percentage
	#	%
Total Public	1,699	100
Region**		
East	493	29
Midwest	455	27
South	457	27
West	292	17
Size of Place		
Cities: central cities in urbanized areas (generally 50,000 or more)	528	31
Suburbs: urbanized areas outside central cities	491	29
Towns: other urban areas (generally 2,500 to 49,000)	290	17
Rural: anything not included above	388	23
Age		
21-24	151	9
25-34	380	23
35-49	438	25
50-64	425	24
65 and over	303	19
Race		
White	1,492	88
Non-white	195	11
Income		
Under $7,000	238	15
$7,000-$14,999	536	31
$15,000-$24,999	554	33
$25,000 and over	310	18
Sex		
Male	1,006	62
Female	690	38

*Subgroup totals do not always come to 1,699 because of some non-response.

**East includes: Connecticut, Delaware, District of Columbia, Maine, Maryland, Massachusetts, New Hampshire, New Jersey, New York, Pennsylvania, Rhode Island, Vermont, and West Virginia.

Midwest includes: Illinois, Indiana, Iowa, Kansas, Michigan, Minnesota, Missouri, Nebraska, North Dakota, Ohio, South Dakota, and Wisconsin.

South includes: Alabama, Arkansas, Florida, Georgia, Kentucky, Louisiana, Mississippi, North Carolina, Oklahoma, South Carolina, Tennessee, Texas, and Virginia.

West includes: Arizona, California, Colorado, Idaho, Montana, Nevada, New Mexico, Oregon, Utah, Washington, and Wyoming.

B. The leadership sample: The leadership sample consisted of a representative cross-section of 212 companies drawn from the Fortune 1250 listing and the *Dun and*

Bradstreet Million Dollar Directory. The sample was stratified and is representative of companies according to the number of people employed.

In each case the Chief Executive Officer was contacted and asked to designate someone who was felt to represent the company's views on pensions and retirement. Interviews were obtained as follows:

Number of Interviews	Position
31	President, Chief Executive Officer
16	Sr. VP or Executive VP
46	VP Personnel, Pensions or Benefits
14	VP Financial
10	Other VPs
65	Managers, Directors
9	Treasurer, Chief Financial Officer, Comptroller
5	Assistant Treasurer
5	Benefit Administrator/Officer
2	Assistant Secretary
1	Benefit Specialist
1	Employee Retirement & Welfare Coordinator
1	Assistant to President
1	Senior Specialist
1	Consultant to Investment Committee
1	General Counsel
3	No Specific Title Given (Blank)

JOHNSON & HIGGINS
COMMENTARY

The study of a social issue as complex as retirement requires a constant effort to avoid losing sight of the main question. It is quite easy to become side-tracked while examining many of the interrelated sub-issues and the mass of facts and opinions which are elements of the overall problem.

Economics, labor force composition, capital formation, demographics, political realities, productivity, inflation, taxation and funding must be considered along with past performance and current attitudes in order to evaluate the potential future directions this issue could take.

For the sake of establishing a framework in which the available information can be organized and evaluated, J&H would hypothesize that:

> A coordinated retirement policy should aim for an adequate retirement income, upon retirement and thereafter for a worker and spouse, taking into account all available sources of income.

This framework specifically excludes the broader question of income transfers based on need without regard to prior employment, length of service or past earnings. While some retired employees may need such assistance, income transfers of this type are not related to retirement per se. It is not possible to provide all perceived social income needs through a retirement system. The question under study should not be obscured by blending it into a larger problem.

The elements of the theorem can be used to arrange available information under the following categories:

What is an Adequate Retirement Income?
- at the time of retirement
- during the period of retirement

What Should the National Policy be Toward Retirement Age?
- employment beyond age 65
- intentions of employees

How Should Retirement Income be Defined and Determined?
- what type of income should be replaced
- should benefits be based on earnings or need

What Should National Policy be Toward . . .?
- personal savings for retirement
- integration of private pensions and Social Security
- portability
- mandatory pensions

How Should Retirement Income Sources be Funded?
- private pension plans
- public plans (for government employees)
- Social Security

What is an Adequate Retirement Income?

Should "adequate" be measured in comparison to pre-retirement spendable income, pre-retirement standard of living, desired standard of living or something less?

The overwhelming majority of employees (89%), retirees (92%) and employers (82%) believe that the post-retirement standard of living should be equal to or better than the pre-retirement standard of living. This goal is optimistic and will become less realistic as the retiree to worker ratio increases in future years and inflation takes its toll.

A more achievable goal would seem to be one where the combined retirement income available from a pension plan and Social Security provides a standard of living somewhere between "comfortable subsistence" and the pre-retirement standard. This would then be supplemented by personal savings and other assets.

The adequacy goal should be defined in terms of a percentage of the spendable after-tax income level shortly before retirement, weighted to favor the lower paid individual. Ideally, the initial benefit would be adjusted, within the constraints of financial feasibility, for post-retirement increases in the cost of living. 93% of employees and retirees and 51% of business leaders believe it is important that pension plan benefits increase as the cost of living goes up.

Even with the more optimistic pre-retirement standard of living in mind, the study shows that 76% of retirees who are receiving pensions claim to have a standard of living which is adequate or more than adequate while only 43% of retirees who do not receive pensions feel the same way.

This means the overall system needs improvement because a substantial minority claim to have a less than adequate standard of living to some degree — 23% of pensioners and 56% of those who are not receiving pension benefits.

These results also highlight the dramatic difference in the standard of living between those retirees who are receiving pensions and those who are not and clearly shows:

(A) Social Security has not, in the aggregate, provided adequate retirement benefits to the American public. The stated intention of the Social Security system initially was to provide only a basic floor of protection.

(B) Pension plans have, to a very large degree, done the job they were designed to do — i.e. bridge the gap between a basic level of Social Security benefits and an adequate standard of living. This is true despite the fact that retiree expectations are high and current retirees have by and large, retired under less generous plans than will future retirees.

The pension system already covers a large majority of employees:

(A) 60% of current workers are covered by private plans (about 7 out of 10 who work in the private sector) and 23% by public employee plans.

(B) Of employees age 50 and over, 62% are covered by private plans and 28% by public plans.

NOTE: There may be some duplication of those covered by private and public plans — e.g. "Double Dippers".

The pension system must be expanded to cover an even larger percentage of employees. The federal government is moving in the right direction by encouraging simplified pension plans and IRA accounts to fill the coverage gap among employees of small employers.

Assuming employees are covered by a pension plan and Social Security, which together provide an adequate standard of living at retirement, there remains the problem of how to maintain this standard in a period of sustained, high-level inflation. 84% of current retirees claim that inflation has reduced their standard of living. We believe that this is a major problem that must be dealt with by the private pension system.

One scenario that pops up as a trial balloon from time to time runs as follows:

(A) Private pension plans cannot keep pace with increases in the cost of living;

(B) Social Security is indexed to the cost of living;

(C) Therefore, we should eliminate private pensions, with their tax "subsidies", and provide all retirement income through Social Security.

We believe the survey shows a number of major defects in this line of thought.

(A) The Social Security system cannot provide the level of benefits needed to maintain an adequate standard of living. Simply maintaining the present levels of replacement ratios would eat up an estimated 21% (excluding Medicare) of covered payroll by the end of the first quarter of the next century. Only 30% of employees and 49% of business leaders agree that the 1977 Amendment increasing taxes was the proper approach. Clearly, the wage-based Social Security tax is approaching an upper limit of tolerance — politically and economically.

(B) Most Americans would not want the Social Security system to provide all their retirement income. Only 17% of current and retired employees would favor this approach. 42% of current employees have hardly any confidence that the Social Security system will be able to pay their benefits when they retire.

(C) The pension system is making a major contribution toward mitigating the impact of inflation. 53% of retired employees who are not receiving pension benefits claim that their standard of living is being seriously reduced. Only 28% of retired employees who are receiving pension benefits are feeling the same degree of impact.

(D) There is a widespread distrust on the part of workers and business leaders in the government's ability to manage Social Security. As an indication of this, 32% of current employees and 37% of business leaders would, if given a choice, get out of the system.

The underlying question is whether a sufficient portion of the real wealth (goods and services) being produced currently can be allocated to maintain the standard of living of current retirees. If the economy can afford this, it can be done through private and public pensions as adequately in the future as this survey shows has been done in the past. If the economy cannot afford this allocation of current wealth, eliminating private pension plans and promising fully adequate and indexed benefits from Social Security or other governmental programs will not work. All that is accomplished is deferral of the cost of current benefits to future generations of wealth producers — at a time when the retiree/worker ratio is beginning to increase. If too much of a burden is shifted to the future, the succeeding generations of workers may simply refuse to honor the "pledges" of their predecessors.

The real problem is inflation — not pension plan adequacy. If the inflation problem itself is not solved, government retirement benefit schemes can only hide and defer the true cost. While pension plans cannot solve the problem of inflation, the private pension industry has developed a number of techniques that mitigate the full impact of inflation on retirement benefits. Plan sponsors should utilize available techniques within the limits of available funds, lest the perceived benefit gap be filled by a federal deficit-financed scheme which would assure continuation of the vicious inflation spiral.

In addition to existing techniques, one new approach to be explored would be to earmark employee contributions to provide some cost-of-living protection as the initial benefit provided by the plan begins to be eroded by inflation. This approach would be more attractive if the employee contributions were deductible for federal and state income tax purposes. The study shows that 68% of plan participants state they would contribute if it increased their retirement benefits.

Johnson & Higgins believes that an employer achieves good results in employee benefits with features that are valued and appreciated by plan participants. Pension plan provisions that come to grips with the inflation problem will address what the survey shows is the principal concern of participants. It is likely that pension plan improvements of this type will be the most effective.

What Should the National Policy be Toward Retirement Age?

The conventional wisdom regarding the impact of the recent amendment to the Age Discrimination Act of 1967 on retirement ages holds that:

- there is a well-established trend toward early retirement.
- changes in the mandatory retirement age will not affect the number of employees who retire before normal retirement age.
- it will have little effect on the percentage of employees who will work beyond normal retirement age.
- the overall impact on pension plans and costs will be minor.

The responses obtained from the employees and retirees themselves cast great doubt on the long-term accuracy of this conventional wisdom. **Only 47% of all current employees (52% of private pension plan participants) say they intend to stop working on or before normal retirement age. Another 8% in both categories intend to retire and take a job with another employer. In addition to this 8%, approximately 41% of employees and 38% of private pension plan participants say they intend to work as long as they can at the same job, a less demanding job or a part-time job.**

This surprising result among active employees correlates with the preferences of retired employees — 46% of whom would prefer to be working now and 53% of whom would have preferred to continue working instead of retiring.

It is not determinable whether most employees will do what they say they intend to do. It does seem abundantly clear that a far greater number of older employees than employers have anticipated will continue in the work force in some capacity.

It is difficult to forecast accurately how this will impact costwise on private retirement income plans. There will be no plan savings for the 60% of plan participants who intend to retire on or before normal retirement age. Unless the plan provides a credit for post age 65 service, there should be a savings for the 17% who intend to remain full time in the same job or in a less demanding job. The 21% who intend to remain in part-time employment will probably represent modest savings only. They would most likely not take part-time work with the same employer if it meant the loss of current pension payments.

The effect of continued employment on the Social Security system will depend on the earnings limitation test, the extra credit for working beyond age 65, additional Social Security taxes paid during "post retirement" employment and any future changes in the retirement age to qualify for full benefits.

With the emergence of a substantial number of employees who intend to remain in employment at the older ages, the demographic shift in the retiree/worker ratio and sustained inflation, a number of approaches will undoubtedly be evaluated by Congress and by employers:

- a gradual deferral of the age at which unreduced pension and Social Security benefits commence

- require additional pension credits for employment beyond age 65

- elimination of inducements for early retirement under private and public pension plans and greater reliance on personnel practices to weed out lagging performers.

How Should Retirement Income be Defined and Determined?

Retirement income from Social Security and pension plans should be limited to the replacement, to a worker and spouse, of income lost because of a permanent removal from the working force by reason of retirement due to age or permanent disability.

The survey showed, however, that eighty-three percent (83%) of both employees and business leaders believe that it is very important or extremely important that a pension plan provide survivor income benefits to the spouse of a deceased employee. This is a proper and desirable benefit for employees who have or could have retired and started receiving benefits.

Nevertheless, we believe that a retirement income system should not be used to provide for other types of income needs not related to retirement — such as death benefits to dependents, health benefits or sick pay. The issue of retirement and retirement income maintenance must be clearly defined and limited if a national policy is to be developed. Interjecting tangential income needs into the retirement issue merely serves to divert attention and funds from the main problem.

If pension plans are mandated to provide pre-retirement death benefits and other types of benefits not specifically related to retirement income, then the primary objective of retirement income maintenance is lost. Furthermore, funds which could have been used to increase retirement income would be diverted to other uses.

Responses from employees and business leaders on the determination of retirement income levels lead to a consensus that:

- Social Security benefits should provide a basic level of retirement income
  (76% of employees and 98% of business leaders).

- this basic Social Security benefit should be related to the worker's previous income or should supplement other retirement income
  (54% of employees and 77% of business leaders).

- pension plan benefits should be based on earnings and length of employment
  (58% of employees and 90% of business leaders).

When asked whether a basic level of retirement income, regardless of pre-retirement income, should be provided

(A) from Social Security,
   only 22% employees and 21% business leaders said yes, and

(B) from pension plans,
   only 28% employees and 5% business leaders thought so.

This consensus reflects a broad structure for determining retirement income benefits.

- a basic level of retirement benefits paid from Social Security geared to prior earnings but with a minimum benefit amount.
- a pension plan benefit based on prior earnings and employment with a supplemental minimum benefit where needed to reinforce the Social Security minimum.

This retirement income would be supplemented by personal savings and other assets. If any benefits are to be payable solely on the basis of need without a relationship to prior earnings they should come from an income-transfer system other than Social Security and should not be confused with the retirement income maintenance supported by payroll taxes and pension plans.

National Policy Issues

The survey shows that 54% of employees believe they should share some responsibility to provide for their retirement income along with the government and/or the employer. A substantial 39% believe the government and/or their employer should bear the whole burden while 7% are not sure.

This 39% who feel that employees have no responsibility for providing for their own retirement income represents a clear danger signal for a national retirement income policy. This attitude is reflected in figures reported in a recent study showing that Americans save far less than citizens of other industrial countries and that the rate of savings is decreasing. In 1967, consumer savings in America totalled 7.5% of consumer after-tax income. This dropped to 5.1% in 1977. All other industrial countries in the report (Canada, Britain, West Germany, France and Japan) showed increases in the savings rates. By 1977 Canada with the lowest rate, was saving 9.8% and Japan, with the highest rate, 21.5%.

The statistics for American savings rates can be attributable to many elements — erosion of purchasing power through inflation, slow-down of the economic growth rate, more comprehensive social programs, lack of tax incentives to save — but the trend confirms a growing unwillingness or inability of Americans to save for their own retirement.

This is a particularly disturbing trend when coupled with a possible peaking of the ability of the Social Security system to raise additional funds by payroll taxes and the ever-present demand on pension plans for increased benefits and cost-of-living protection.

Johnson & Higgins feels that any long-range policy for a retirement income system must re-emphasize the responsibility of the employee to share in the cost of providing his own retirement security. This policy should be supported by tax incentives for individual retirement plans and for employee contributions to employer-sponsored pension plans.

In response to the question of whether Social Security benefits should be taken into account when determining the amount to be received from a pension plan — that is, whether private pension plan benefits should be coordinated ("integrated") with Social Security benefits — 55% of all employees and 22% of business leaders said no. 60% of workers covered by private plans and 67% of those covered by public plans said no.

Interestingly enough, however, when asked how the post-retirement standard of living should compare with the pre-retirement standard of living, 81% of employees and 82% of business leaders replied that they should be about the same. (Only 8% of employees and no business leaders believed it should be higher).

118

This combination of responses is contradictory and shows a lack of understanding of the interplay of Social Security with pension plans. If the consensus is that the post-retirement standard of living should be relatively the same as the pre-retirement standard of living then both Social Security benefits and pension plan benefits must be taken into account and coordinated.

For example, consider a pension plan which provides a benefit of $10 per month for each year of employment (a typical benefit level for a "non-integrated" plan). An average employee who retires in 1980 with 30 years of service would receive an annual benefit of $3,600. When added to the amount ($7,973) of Social Security benefit payable to a worker and spouse (assuming the worker earned the average wage covered by Social Security, about $11,000 in 1979), this produces a combined (integrated) retirement income of $11,573. This means a total income of about 105% of pre-retirement gross income and 128% of pre-retirement spendable income.

Now consider a pension plan which integrates directly in the plan formula. For example, a plan that provides 50% of the final five-year average pay reduced by 50% of the primary Social Security benefit after 30 years of service. The same worker earning the average covered Social Security wage would receive a plan benefit of $2,343 plus $7,973 from Social Security for a total "integrated" retirement income of $10,316 — about 94% of pre-retirement gross income and 115% of pre-retirement spendable income.

The point is that Social Security benefits do exist whether taken into account or not. Only by taking them into account in designing pension plan benefits can a combined retirement income program be produced that meets the standard of living objective. It should also be noted that the combined retirement income favors lower-paid employees because it replaces a higher percentage of pay at the lower income levels.

Another point of considerable interest on the subject of sources of retirement income arises from attitudes on portability. Thirty-four percent (34%) of employees would prefer to have their old pension plan hold the accrued benefits if they were to change jobs; 29% would prefer that the funds be transferred to their new plan; 31% would prefer that the funds be transferred to an individual account, like an IRA.

Only 2% of employees would want their funds transferred to the federal government pending their retirement. This chilling lack of enthusiasm for transferring private pension funds to the federal government coincides with the need to maintain these accumulated assets in the capital-generating private sector.

The issue of mandatory pension plans is one that will take considerable study. While 80% of employees feel that every employer should be required to provide a reasonable pension plan for his employees, only 33% of business leaders agree. As previously mentioned, the survey shows that for employees near retirement (age 50 and over), 62% are covered by private pension plans and 28% by public pension plans — leaving relatively few employees without pension coverage at retirement. Johnson & Higgins believes that the private pension system is an essential part of an overall retirement income system and that coverage of employees in private pension plans is to be fully encouraged. But a mandated "minimum pension plan" law could result in many small businesses closing up entirely. We think that national policy should continue to provide tax incentives for employees of small employers to establish individual retirement accounts and should develop incentives for small employers to establish pension plans. A variety of vehicles will be needed to maximize coverage among this group.

How Should Retirement Income Sources be Funded?

Private Pension Plans

The "broken promise" atmosphere of the early 1970's seems to have cleared. 93% of plan participants have confidence that their plan will pay their promised benefits and 78% of plan participants are basically satisfied with the way their plans are designed and administered.

The funding status of private pension plans is not a major concern for most companies, does not impose a burdensome cost on employers, and pension plans are, for the most part, adequately funded to pay the promised benefits.

Survey results show that the contribution to employee pension plans, including profit sharing and thrift plans averaged 11% of payroll for 193 responding companies. A separate survey conducted by Johnson & Higgins among a very large sample of Fortune 500 companies shows an average contribution for pension plans (excluding in most cases profit sharing and thrift plans) of 8% of payroll during 1977 fiscal years. This same J&H survey showed pension costs, on the average, to be 12.4% of pretax profits.

The Harris survey shows that 98% of business leaders think their plans are adequately funded. However, 16% consider unfunded liabilities as a major concern for their company. The J&H survey shows that 27% of the sample of Fortune 500 companies had no unfunded vested liabilities at all; three-quarters had unfunded vested liabilities of less than 10% of net worth and only 5% had unfunded vested liabilities of 30% or more of net worth. Unfunded liabilities (vested plus non-vested) were less than 10% of net worth for 52% of the sample of Fortune 500 companies. There were only 9% with unfunded liabilities of 30% or more of net worth.

The overall conclusion is that private pension plans are, on the whole, adequately funded and are likely to remain so. The minimum funding requirements of ERISA and the guarantees of the Pension Benefit Guaranty Corporation are additional safeguards.

Public Pension Plans

There is substantial agreement that public pension plans should be funded on the same basis as private pension plans. This opinion was expressed by 66% of all current and retired employees, 69% of employees covered by public plans and 90% of business leaders. In our view, national policy should be directed at requiring minimum funding standards for public pension plans. It is hoped that any constitutional issues can be overcome in addressing this issue.

Social Security

Social Security funding problems continue to be of major concern. The American public does understand that benefits are being paid from current Social Security taxes — only 8% labor under the formerly widespread delusion that their taxes are set aside in their own account. **There is a crisis of confidence among employees which leads to doubt that the Social Security system will pay their benefits when they retire.** This attitude is most pronounced at the younger ages but, in total, 42% of current employees (over 50% of those under age 35) have hardly any confidence in receiving these benefits. This minimum confidence in receiving benefits is matched by a lack in confidence that future working generations will be willing to pay higher Social Security taxes to support those benefits — again 41% of current and retired employees have hardly any confidence. The assessment here is probably right on target as witnessed by the present stiffening of resistance to the tax increases mandated by the 1977 Amendments.

This reluctance of the American public to fund Social Security benefits by sharply increased payroll taxes is already leading to suggestions for alternate means of funding to support present and even increased benefit levels. Forty-seven percent (47%) of employees believe that funding for Social Security benefits should come partly from sources other than payroll taxes. Only 17% of business leaders agree with this attitude. Alternate sources include the possibility of general revenue tapping or, as some have suggested, the imposition of a value-added type of tax. Of course, it is difficult to see how general revenue can be a viable solution when, even in the best of times, the government manages to run high deficits. A value-added tax would be inflationary, just like diverting general revenues, and would merely mask the real problem — the benefits are too rich to pay to the demographic wave of future beneficiaries. A heavy use of non-payroll taxation could result in irresponsible election year goodies and perhaps the eventual demise of Social Security.

Conclusion

Johnson & Higgins is of the opinion that the real answer lies in the proper balancing of benefits and funding. Social Security benefits should be limited to a basic level of retirement benefits and funding by payroll taxes. It is not possible or practical to provide adequate retirement income to all Americans through the Social Security system. This fact should become a fundamental tenet of national policy. Responsibility for benefits over and above a basic level should be transferred to employers and employees. Expansion of pension plan coverage should be encouraged. Minimum funding standards should be applied to public as well as private plans.

The national confirmation of such a policy will go a long way toward solving our capital formation needs and will in turn help to assure the productive growth of our economy.

We urge the policymakers to move to this logical solution.